Erica,

Happy Birthday, I hope this book
will add to your faith in the Lord.

Prayer and Faith:
The Life
of Dr. Tom Williams

Copyright © 2009
Dr. Tom Williams

First Printing – March 2009
Second Printing – February 2012

ISBN: 978-0-9819603-1-9

All Scriptures used in this book are from the King James Bible.

To order more of these books and other materials
by Dr. Williams, please call or write:

TOM WILLIAMS' WORLDWIDE MINISTRIES
P.O. Box 187 • Greenville, Indiana 47124
Phone: (812) 923-7092
Fax: (812) 923-7093
Web site: www.twwm1.com
e-mail: tomwilliams@twwm1.com

Dedication

WITH ALL OF MY HEART, I dedicate this book to my Heavenly Father, to His Son, the Lord Jesus Christ, Who is my Saviour, and to His blessed Holy Spirit, Who is my constant companion.

Thank You, Father, for hearing my prayers all through the years. Thank You for the Lord Jesus Christ and that His precious blood rent the veil in the Temple from top to bottom and opened to us the throne of grace. Thank You that He and the Holy Spirit make intercession for us. Thank You for the gift of faith that You have given me that I might join it with prayer and behold Your power.

With all my love,

Your son Tom

To My Wife Jeannine

THANK YOU FOR BEING WILLING to marry a battle-scarred old soldier and love him like a young hero. Your countless hours of typing as I dictated this book, your patience in reading and rewriting it over and over, plus your sweet spirit as I unfolded my heart about two other marriages have swelled my love for you beyond description.

Thank you, Darling!

Jeannine Williams

Love,

Tom

Acknowledgments

I WANT TO SAY THANK YOU to my four children, Tim, Phyllis, Paul, and Penny, and their families, for their love and care. Thank you for knowing and believing that our Heavenly Father doesn't make any mistakes.

I want to thank all of the pastors and churches in America and around the world for their help through 48 years of evangelism. I do not know how to fully express my gratitude to you for your prayers in all of my trials.

I praise the Lord for Dr. Jack Hyles, Dr. Jack Schaap, and the members of First Baptist Church of Hammond, Indiana, for loving me in a unique and wonderful way. Their help in getting this book ready for publication has been nothing short of sacrifice.

May the message and miracles of this book be a return on your investment in my life.

– Dr. Tom Williams

Table of Contents

Foreword by Tim Williams 11

Introduction 13

CHAPTER ONE
My Conversion 15

CHAPTER TWO
My Call 21

CHAPTER THREE
Learning Faith in the Early Years of Evangelism 33

CHAPTER FOUR
The Next Step of Faith 55

CHAPTER FIVE
The Door That Faith Opened 63

CHAPTER SIX
The Thrills and Trials of Motor Home Life 75

CHAPTER SEVEN
Prayer, the Twin Sister of Faith .83

CHAPTER EIGHT
Answers From Heaven 91

CHAPTER NINE
God's Amazing Salvation 119

PRAYER AND FAITH:

The Life of Dr. Tom Williams

CHAPTER TEN
    The Storm of Our Life 135

CHAPTER ELEVEN
    Years of Sustaining Faith 143

CHAPTER TWELVE
    Abundant Grace 157

CHAPTER THIRTEEN
    Channels of Blessing 165

CHAPTER FOURTEEN
    The New Beginning 175

Foreword

HOW FASCINATING FOR THE "SONS of the prophets" to have lived with Elisha of the Old Testament. They must have been so blessed to have seen the mighty miracles of his ministry. Timothy and Titus, no doubt, were thrilled to have traveled with the Apostle Paul. As that great missionary wrote Scripture, planted churches, and battled the enemies of the Gospel, they must have been stirred and molded to serve Christ.

Truly it has been my privilege to journey with Dr. Tom Williams as a great preacher and as my parent for over a half century. During these years, he has always been my hero. We have shared the heights and depths of life together. Family time allowed me to see him beyond the pulpit as a husband, a father, a cowboy, an athlete, a humorist, and a poet. In the pulpit he has been ablaze for the Gospel through powerful preaching and a ringing call for revival. Multitudes of preachers and church members have sought his counsel and prayers. His convictions, vision for strengthened marriages, passion for lost souls, and trust in God's provision have remained unshakable. As you read his life, you will be inspired, as I have been, both to hope during troubled times and to hunger for the power of the Almighty.

Regarding this man of God, this fervent evangelist, and his ministry, may I share three observations. First, he is a man of faith. All Christians are called to have faith, but some seem to be blessed with a greater measure of it (Romans 12:3, 6). My father has exercised his measure of faith with astounding impact! Secondly, he is a man of prayer. He has a prayer *life*—not just a prayer *time*. From my childhood to the present, I have observed him on his knees for long seasons earnestly pleading with God. And, oh, the answers to prayer! Finally, he is a man of compassion. Always a stalwart for holiness, he has graciously exhibited mercy to prodigal sons and straying sheep. An amazingly tender heart has aptly earned him the description of "preacher to the hurting."

I am greatly honored to have been given this opportunity to introduce my father's life story to you. After all these years, I still want to be like him when I grow up.

– Tim Williams

Introduction

I WAS BORN THE YOUNGEST OF 14 children to Mr. and Mrs. Ross Williams of Snyder, Texas. I was reared on a farm and ranch operation and grew up loving the cowboy life. My father raised horses and mules and then sold them to the U.S. Cavalry during World War II. Our home was a place of tremendous activity with people coming and going continuously.

Many times I had to sleep on a pallet, which in those days was simply a quilt on the floor. The house was crowded; however, it was a place of happiness and joy. I remember so well the laughter, the jokes played on one another, and always the great love that our family had for one another.

I am thankful for the integrity of my father and of my grandfather who instilled in me the character to pay my bills and do my best at any job—whatever it might be. I am so thankful for the godly prayers of my mother and grandmother who spent hours reading the Bible and praying. My mother prayed earnestly that one of her nine sons would be a preacher. I had two brothers that in later years preached some, but I was the only one called into full-time service for our Lord.

In my years of growing up, I would come home, many times late at night, to see my mother sitting at the kitchen table reading her Bible. In my mind I can still vividly picture her doing so. My mother's love was so unusual in its depth and longsuffering. Though she has been dead for 40 years, I still weep every time I read her will. In her will she willed us her love, which was a God-given love. I am so grateful to the Lord that He gave me a portion of her love for people and for my Lord. I am sure that I am in the ministry and that much of what God has accomplished through me is largely because of my mother's prayers.

CHAPTER ONE

❦

My Conversion

I WAS CONVERTED IN DECEMBER OF 1955, from a life of deep sin and wickedness. Being the youngest of nine boys, I learned many things which led me into a wicked life. I remember smoking coffee grounds, cedar bark, grapevines, and dried cotton leaves from the time I was six years old. My father, being a very moral man, would discipline us, but smoking held a grip on my life over the next 14 years. I tasted my first drink of liquor when I was ten years old, and I drank until I was converted at 20 years of age. My mouth was so filthy that cowboys and oil field workers would ask me to stop the pickup I was driving and let them walk. I danced several nights a week to country and western music and sold pornography to help put myself through high school.

My reputation was so ungodly that many parents did not want their daughters even to be around me. Because of my memory of these things, I plead so hard with young people today to be so careful of what they watch and hear. I don't want even one to have a lifetime of such memories as mine.

My work in the oil fields led me to California at the age of 17 because the pay there was much higher than in Texas. There I met my first wife, Wanda Claud, and we were married in Texas on July 23, 1954. She was a godly young lady, and I deceived her into marrying me by going to church and pretending to be a Christian. I had joined the church when I was 14 years old and pretended to be saved

~ 15 ~

to make my mother happy. I had become very efficient at deceiving people into believing that I had been converted.

As I look back, it scares me for so many others who have a name of being a Christian but have nothing in their life that testifies of a conversion. Please understand that old saying, "All that glitters is not gold." I could quote Scripture, I could pray, and I could talk to people about the Lord, but those things do not cause a person to be born again. I led my wife away from the things of the Lord and into the things of the world.

Wanda and I welcomed our son Tim into the world on September 21, 1955, and soon after his birth, we moved from my hometown of Snyder, Texas, to San Angelo, Texas. As I look back, I see the hand of God moving so mightily in bringing me to Him. I am not bragging, but in every job that I have ever had I was considered one of the finest workers; however, for no reason, I was laid off from my job in Snyder, and a very similar job working in the oil field was offered to me in San Angelo.

I was very close to my family and normally would have refused to move, but I needed a job to take care of my wife and new baby son, so we moved to San Angelo. I had no idea we would only live there for five months, but the Lord knew that was where I was to be converted.

One day while living in San Angelo, two men from the San Angelo Baptist Temple knocked on our door to share the plan of salvation with my wife and me and invited us to church. I was able to convince them that we were both Christians and that we would consider coming. We visited a couple of times over the next few months. The Spirit of God was faithful to use His Word to begin to convict me of my lost condition: I constantly saw myself lost and bound for the flames of Hell. I began to lose sleep because of the conviction of the Lord. I would wake up at night in a cold sweat and my heart filled with fear. However, my pride kept me from making a clean break for the Lord because I feared what people would think and what my wife would think of me if I told them I had been lying all the time.

On a Saturday afternoon during the first week of December 1955, I was on my way to an oil drilling rig to deliver supplies. While crossing a dry river bed, the Spirit of God spoke to my heart and said, "Tom, it is time for you to be saved before I have to do something drastic in your life." I stopped the pickup right in the middle of the dry river bed, jumped out, and fell on my knees. I promised God if He would keep me alive until the next morning, I would take my wife and baby to church and be saved.

The next morning I took my wife and son with me to the San Angelo Baptist Temple. The longer the pastor spoke, the more a battle raged in my heart. Satan was telling me that I better not get saved. He said, "The cigarettes in your pocket will have to be put away forever. The liquor in your refrigerator will have to be poured out and never replaced. You will never be able to tell another dirty joke. The books you read will have to be burned. You will no longer be able to listen to the country-western music you love. All your friends will laugh at you and not want anything else to do with you or your family."

The Holy Spirit was saying to me, "If the Lord Jesus comes today, you will be left. Wanda and the baby will go to Heaven. The whole family sitting in front of you will go to Heaven, but your family will be separated." Then He emphatically said, "You told Me you would get saved if I kept you alive until this morning."

I was fighting such a war that sweat was rolling down my face, and much of my body was drenched in sweat as if I had been standing in a shower of water. All of a sudden I could not stand it any longer. I stepped out in the aisle and began to run to the front of the church. The pastor was not giving an invitation to come to Christ; he was in the middle of his message. I ran right up on the platform and grabbed him saying, "Preacher, I have to be saved, and I mean right now!" I think I probably scared him out of ten years of his life. However, he stopped preaching, and we knelt at the altar, and he led me to Christ. He showed me from Scripture that I was a sinner and that I had to have a Saviour. He showed me that if I really believed in my heart that Christ was the Lord, that He died for me, that He rose again on the third day, and if I confessed this with my mouth, that I would be saved. I did this, and the Lord gloriously converted me to Himself.

I did not look around, but my wife came to rededicate her life to Christ, and 25 other people came for salvation. God shook the whole church through what happened to me that morning.

As I walked out of the church that day, the cigarettes in my pocket felt like the *Encyclopedia Britannica*. I could not wait to get rid of them. As I wadded them up and threw them in the trash, I said, "Camel, I have carried you as far as I'm going to. From now on, you'll have to walk." We drove home that day, and I took the beer, malt liquor, and all of the other liquor out of our refrigerator and poured them down the sink.

I tell folks that it was probably the cleanest the drain had ever been. All of the ungodly books were burned, and my music was all changed. I had a love of country and western music like young people today have for rock 'n' roll music. My friends also changed. Those who knew me best either got saved from our testimony or wanted nothing else to do with us.

I thank God that He made a clean sweep in my life. Sunday night my family and I were back in church. Monday I went to work, and I asked the men with whom I worked what they had heard come out of my mouth. They answered, "You have asked, so we will tell you that you have the filthiest mouth of any man we have ever known."

I said, "I got saved yesterday, and from now on my mouth will speak of Christ and what He has done for me." I am so thankful that, as I write this book over 53 years later, that promise has been true.

My Call

I HAD BEEN SAVED JUST TWO weeks when God called me to preach the Gospel of the Lord Jesus Christ. The Lord used the same pastor who had led me to Christ to also lead me to understand that God wanted me to preach. The pastor said to me, "I don't know why I am saying this to you; I have never said it to any man. I know beyond the shadow of a doubt that God wants you to preach."

I replied, "Pastor, I told you what kind of life I was saved from, and now two weeks later you want me to preach?"

He said, "I believe it so much that I am going to have you preach Wednesday night."

I said to him, "Are you sure you have not lost your mind?"

He said he was certain that this was of the Lord. I asked him to please pray for me that the Lord would give me the message He wanted me to preach. I remembered a verse in the Bible that my mother often quoted about getting in your closet and praying. Matthew 6:6 said if you did pray, the Lord was sure to hear you, and not only would He hear you, but He would also reward you openly.

I went home and removed my wife's sewing machine and all our shoes from the closet. I then got in the closet with my Bible, put it on the floor, and knelt down over it, asking God to give me a message. The first message that I ever preached was from Luke 7 on the faith of the centurion. I had no way of knowing that this would be a message that would depict my life for all the coming years.

I preached about 20 minutes and had many compliments on the message. The people said that it was very good, and I am certain that they were very kind in their remarks. Speaking in public was not difficult for me as I had been president of my high school's Future Farmers of America chapter. I had also been on the debate team while in high school. The difficulty was that I was now handling the eternal Word of God. I never lost the thrill of that moment of declaring "...*Thus saith the Lord.*" I now possessed a driving desire to preach every time there was an opportunity. God wonderfully blessed me with a craving to know His Word. He also gave me a tremendous memory when He formed me in my mother's womb. My memory has been an indescribable blessing to me through the years.

Two weeks after I had preached my first sermon, the pastor asked me to begin to teach a junior boys' Sunday school class. I never felt so unworthy in all my life as I did telling these little boys how to live for the Lord Jesus Christ. I suppose in the over 53 years of being in the ministry that the one question I have been asked most is, "Brother Williams, how were you called to preach?" I have never thought that anyone else had to be called in the same way that I was.

We see in the Bible many men called to serve God, yet none of those calls are the same.

- Genesis 6 gives an account of the call of Noah, who was asked by the Lord to build an ark and, while doing so, to preach the Gospel. In II Peter 2:5 God says, "*And spared not the old world, but saved Noah the eighth person, a preacher of righteousness, bringing in the flood upon the world of the ungodly.*"
- Genesis 12:1 says, "*Now the LORD had said unto Abram, Get thee out of thy country, and from thy kindred, and from thy father's house, unto a land that I will shew thee.*" Hebrews 11:8 says, "*By faith Abraham, when he was called to go out into a*

place which he should after receive for an inheritance, obeyed; and he went out, not knowing whither he went."

- In I Samuel 16 God called David through the prophet Samuel. The Lord sent Samuel to anoint one of the sons of Jesse to be king in Saul's place. God did not tell Samuel which son of Jesse, but Samuel knew it had to be David when none of Jesse's other sons had been chosen.
- In I Kings 19 God used the prophet Elijah to call Elisha into His work.
- In the New Testament we see the Saviour, the Lord Jesus Christ, call 12 men. Some were called from fishing, some from tax collecting, and some from other occupations.
- He then calls 70 about whom we know little.
- Probably the most unique call in the New Testament is the call of Saul of Tarsus in Acts 9.

In 1 Samuel 16:7 the Bible says, "*...the LORD seeth not as man seeth; for man looketh on the outward appearance, but the LORD looketh on the heart.*" God's calling is not always to the tallest, to the most handsome, or to the most gifted, for God sees not as man sees. As you read about the different calls of these men, you will notice the diversity of their circumstances, their situations, and their backgrounds. You will also see that most of them were asked to do something extraordinary. Many of them suffered great losses as well. It would be foolish of me or anyone else to think that the God of Heaven Who never made two fingerprints alike, or two leaves or two grains of sand or two snowflakes, would have to call any two men the same way. As men of God, let us pray one for another in our calling that we will glorify our Heavenly Father and our blessed Lord Jesus Christ through the power of the Holy Ghost.

The Lord continued to lead in my newfound life in Christ. We had been in San Angelo just five months when my wife's mother in Los Angeles, California, fell and very severely broke her right leg. My wife was the only daughter, and her father asked if we could come to California and take care of her mom for the next six months. After praying, we decided that it was God's will for our lives at that time.

I was able to get a job in the oil fields of California to provide for my family, and I began to teach a Sunday school class at the church we began to attend. Soon I was made Sunday school superintendent. I also met two young men in the church who also had been called to preach, and the three of us began to study the Word of God together, challenging each other to memorize Scripture. This was a very profitable time for me as these men also knew where the local opportunities were to preach in Los Angeles.

I began to preach twice a week at skid-row missions in Los Angeles and San Pedro. Over the next four years, I began to receive invitations to preach at youth rallies, men's meetings, and at summer camps. We would also go to preach in bus stations, at Pershing Square, and on street corners in downtown Los Angeles. Pershing Square is the "Mars Hill" of California. It was the place where anyone who had a philosophy and wanted to debate it would meet.

During my four years of lay preaching, Wanda went home to be with the Lord following the birth of our second child, Sheryl Dee. We were on our way to the hospital when Wanda spoke to me and said, "If I die having this baby, I would appreciate you and the children living with my dad and mom."

"Please don't talk that way," I answered her. "You're 23 years old, and we have our lives before us."

I do not know whether or not the Lord had given her a premonition that she was going to die. Wanda, in fact, had a very difficult time with the birth of Sheryl Dee, which drained her of her strength. When our little girl was finally delivered, the doctors informed us that she was born with spina bifida. I tried the best I could to comfort Wanda's heart that this little girl would not be coming home with us.

Sheryl Dee was born in 1958 when not much was known about spina bifida, and so little could be done for her. The doctors told me that the Los Angeles General Hospital was the only hospital in the L. A. area that could care for Sheryl. He then asked me to drive my precious little daughter, wrapped in a receiving blanket, to the L. A. General Hospital and place her in their care. I believe following the request of that doctor was the most difficult task that I had ever done.

The L. A. General Hospital was like a jungle of people, with patients lying in the hallways who had been shot, stabbed, raped, or had been victims of car wrecks, along with all other sorts of unimaginable cases. I handed Sheryl to a nurse, turned, and walked away with tears streaming down my face and my heart broken. As I write this book 51 years later, I can remember so vividly the trial of my faith in that hour.

I took Wanda home from the hospital after four days. We had been home for eight days when Wanda's body began to swell unbelievably. I called the doctor, and he said, "It is toxic shock poisoning." He gave me a prescription, telling me to get Wanda on it immediately. He also told me that she would begin to lose large amounts of water, which would cause the swelling to go down. However, she could not keep the medicine down, and immediately she began to worsen. I called the doctor again, telling him what was occurring. He told me to call an ambulance and get her to the hospital as soon as possible.

Once we were in the hospital and the doctor had examined my wife, he informed me that her kidneys were failing and the matter was very serious. The physicians tried everything available to counteract her situation, but to no avail. I had taken Wanda to the hospital on Thursday, and on Saturday I was told she had a 50/50 chance of living. Of course, we were praying day and night.

Sunday morning the doctor told me that Wanda now only had a 20 percent chance of living. As the morning ticked away, she grew worse. Sometime right after lunch, I went out to our car, got down on my knees on the floorboard between the front and back seats to tell the Lord that I did not understand everything, but if He wanted Wanda to go Home to Glory, that I would understand and that I would serve Him regardless. I walked back into the hospital to find that Wanda had gone Home to Glory with tremendous convulsions and seizure activity.

The nurse who was with her when she died stopped me at the door of the room and said, "You do not want to see her like she is right now." As the nurse described to me the whole situation, I was thankful to God that He had her there to keep me from entering the room.

The next 24 hours were filled with tremendous emotions as I told our little two and one-half year old son that his mother had gone to Heaven. I also had to make phone calls to both of our families that my sweet wife had been called away by the Lord.

Then there were the funeral arrangements. Having talked to so many people over the years, I certainly agree that choosing the casket is difficult. The Lord gave amazing grace, and I will always be so grateful for my pastor who practically lived with me during those days.

Just as soon as we could, Tim and I went to live with Wanda's parents, Mr. and Mrs. E. B. Claud. We continued to live with them until I remarried the following year. Tim's reaction to his mother's death was a heartrending time. Every night as he and I went to bed, he would cry, "I want my mother. I want my mother." I would hold him very close and try to help him understand that one day we would see her again in God's Heaven. It also became my duty and my privilege every afternoon following work to drive across Los Angeles and sit at the bedside of little Sheryl, who lived four months and twenty days following her birth. She was paralyzed from the hole in her spine downward, and she could move only her hands because her head had grown so large that she could not turn it. I would put my hand through the crib, and she would grasp and hold my finger. During one of these times before her death, the Lord seemed to say to me, "Tom, do you love Sheryl?"

I answered, "Yes, Sir."

He then said, "She is very ugly, isn't she?"

I replied, "Yes, Sir."

He asked me, "Do you love her as much as you love Tim?"

I answered, "Yes, I do—maybe even a little bit more."

He spoke yet again and said, "Tom, I'm going to take Sheryl home to Heaven, but I don't want you to ever forget what she looks like. Just as Sheryl's illness warped her body, sin had done that to your soul, and yet, I loved you and sent My Son to die for you." At that time the Lord broke my heart to love sinners to Christ.

∽◌◌∾

Seeing the tremendous need that Tim had for a mother and my own need for a wife, I began to pray that the Lord would bring someone special who could love both of us. The Lord did so in a unique way by allowing me to meet a beautiful young lady, Pamela James, through my first wife's brother.

I had taken Tim to play with his cousins. Because of the kind of ministry my brother-in-law had, he conducted several vacation Bible schools each summer. Names of volunteer teenagers were drawn from various places to go and help with the vacation Bible schools, and Pam's name had been drawn to go and help my brother-in-law.

She was there the day I took Tim to see his cousins. I was drawn to her beauty as soon as I saw her and yet realized that she was very young. However, the Lord said to me, "Tom, this young lady is your answer to prayer."

"But, Lord," I said, "she sure is young." (Pam was 16 at that time, and I was 23.) The Lord said, "If you don't like the one I picked, then you better get your own."

I replied, "No, Sir, I want the one You want."

I went up one more time to see Pam at my brother-in-law's house, and I said to her, "I think it would be good if I would contact your folks and explain my situation to them to see how they would feel about a 23-year-old man with a son dating their daughter." I called Pam's folks, and they told me that Pam had called and told them about me. Pam's folks were wonderful Christians, and they said, "Because you are a Christian and you are trying to do right about our daughter, when Pam arrives back home, we want you to come and spend the day with us."

I did that, and at the end of the day, they said, "Why don't you and Pam go out for a little while together." We drove a little ways into the country and sat in the car with the dome lights on reading the Bible and praying when I told Pam that I was not a high school boy looking for a date. I was a young man looking for a wife, as well as someone who would love my son as her own.

As we were reading and praying, something very comical happened. A car drove up behind us with red lights spinning round and round. A deputy sheriff got out of that car, walked up to my car, and motioned for me to roll down the window. He said, "Okay, what's going on here?"

I answered, "We are reading the Bible and praying and asking God for His will for our lives." I thought the man would faint.

He stuttered, almost choked, and then said, "I have never caught anyone doing that before."

Every weekend following that time, I began to drive 100 miles one way to see Pam. After several months, I asked Pam to become my wife. She wonderfully accepted my proposal, and it seemed as though my life was absolutely renewed.

After we had become engaged, I took Tim with me each weekend so that he would learn to love Pam and a bond would grow between them. Pam and I were very concerned about how this would work. It only took three visits for us to know God's hand was certainly upon our becoming husband and wife. Tim and I always left early Sunday mornings to drive back to attend our own church as I was Sunday school superintendent. This third Sunday morning as we were preparing to leave, I said to Tim, "It's time to go, Son."

Tim never talked back to me, but that day he said, "I'm not going."

I quickly answered, "What did you say?"

He said, "I am going to stay with Mother because I love her more." God had given us another miracle!

Pam and I were married July 10, 1959, and God gave us our first child together on July 23, 1960, a blessed little girl whom we named Phyllis. God worked a mighty miracle that day in teaching me faith and dependence upon Him. When Pam was in the hospital laboring to give birth to Phyllis, I received an emergency telephone call while I was at work saying that Pam's blood had tested Rh negative. The doctor told me I needed to come immediately to the hospital to be tested for compatibility. If my blood tested Rh positive, the doctors would possibly need to exchange the baby's blood at birth. In those days it was very crucial to have the correct blood type.

I asked the doctor, "What type of blood would be best for my blood to test?"

He replied that it would be wonderful if I too was Rh negative. "Only about 15 percent of people test negative," he added.

PRAYER AND FAITH:

The Life of Dr. Tom Williams

When I told the doctor, "I will pray as I drive to the hospital, and I will believe God to make my blood to be negative as well," he said, "You can't do that! That won't work." However, when my blood was tested, the results indicated that I was Rh negative. The doctor could not believe it. The Lord is so good and so powerful.

In the interval between my wives, the company that I was working for had a layoff, and I was one who was laid off. Immediately the Lord, in answer to prayer, gave me a much better job with the Coca-Cola Bottling Company of Los Angeles. Pam and I had been married almost two years when the Lord began to work in my heart to preach full-time. I was begging the Lord to let me be an evangelist, and the Lord spoke to my heart saying, "Tom, when you preach twice in a row, your tonsils swell up so bad you can't talk," so He directed me to have them removed.

I asked for two weeks off from Coke to have this operation done, but when the doctor looked at my tonsils, he said, "It will take two weeks just to get them operable." However, God worked a miracle, and in four days they were ready to come out, which dumfounded the doctor.

While I was recuperating, Coca-Cola Bottling Company in Los Angeles went on strike for the first time in their history, and when I went back to work, I was required by the union to walk the picket line. I had been walking the picket line for nearly three hours when the Lord spoke to my heart and said, "I don't want you to picket Coke; I want you to preach Christ. It is time for you to go and be an evangelist." I went in to my boss's office and told him I would be leaving because God had called me to be an evangelist. God had blessed me tremendously with the company, and they were moving me up the ladder as fast as possible.

My boss said, "Tom, you can't quit! We're planning to take you to the top of the company."

I explained that I did not have a choice as God had made it very plain out on the street that I was to go. He asked me where I was going to preach, and I said, "I don't know." He also asked me how much pay I would receive, and again I answered, "I don't know." He looked at me very seriously and said, "Tom, you'll be back in six months looking for a job. I will put you back into the company as though you had never left."

I thanked him very kindly and said, "Sir, I will never be back." That morning I walked out into a life of faith, which at the time of this writing has lasted 48 years.

CHAPTER THREE

Learning Faith in the Early Years of Evangelism

THE MORNING I QUIT THE Coca-Cola Bottling Company, I immediately drove home. When I walked into the house, Pam asked, "What are you doing home?"

I replied, "Evangelists come home all during the day."

Mystified by my reply, she asked, "Who comes home during the day?"

I answered, "An evangelist."

She said, "You didn't quit your job?"

I answered, "Yes, I did. While I was walking the picket line today, God called me into full-time work as an evangelist."

She asked me, "How are we going to live?"

I replied, "By faith." I am sure that her mind was on the money that we owed, as well as the normal family expenses. I had a tremendous debt left from the deaths of Wanda and Sheryl Dee. Both funerals and the four months and twenty-day stay in the hospital for Sheryl had developed into an enormous bill.

Many young preachers have the advantage of a father who is a pastor or someone else in the family who is in the ministry. Many of them also have attended Bible college, and their college is willing to recommend them. I had none of these contacts to open doors for me. I could understand somewhat the insecurity that gripped Pam's heart that day, but the one great overwhelming security I had was that I knew without question that God had called me. I clung to the verse in I Thessalonians 5:24 which says, *"Faithful is he that calleth you, who also will do it."*

I believe I can honestly say that I had not one doubt that God in His sovereignty would provide. I had learned through reading the lives of great men who prayed for hours a day that God honors those who pray. I was already praying an hour and a half to two hours a day, and now I would be able to increase that time. I began to pray several hours a day and study and wait upon the Lord to open doors for me to go preach.

I remember so well at the end of the first week how my wife came into the room where I was praying and studying and said to me, "Mr. Evangelist, did you know the rent is due, the car payment is due, and we need to buy groceries?"

I answered her, "Yes, I know about all of those things."

"What are we going to do?"

"We are going to live by faith," I stated.

Well into the second week of praying and waiting for the Lord to give me a place to preach, a businessman came to our door. He said, "Tom, I have checked your sales record with Coca-Cola, and it is tremendous. I'm here today to offer you a job with our corporation, making more money than you ever made in your life."

"I am very honored that you would ask me and offer me such a wonderful job making so much money," I told him. "But I am a full-time evangelist and cannot work for you."

After he had left, my wife walked into the room and half-teasing and half-serious said to me, "I'll tell you what you are; you are a full-time nut." In some ways the job offer was tempting; yet I knew if I didn't win the battle now, I never would. I had already passed one of the great temptations of my life when one of my brothers offered me a ranch operation in Texas, raising and training quarter horses. You will have to understand that, for me, I would rather ride a good horse than eat when I'm hungry.

Approximately three days after I had turned down this job, the West Coast superintendent of the American Sunday School Union, Bob Bunell, came to see me. He said, "Tom, your in-laws have told me of God's call upon your life. I am going to be meeting with about a dozen of our missionaries from Northern California and the state of Nevada this coming Tuesday. They have many little churches and Sunday schools in rural areas. If you will come to Placerville, California, I will give you 15 minutes to tell them of your burden to preach. They may or may not ask you to come."

I told him, "I will be there, the Lord willing." We still did not have any money, but I had a Chevron gas card and a Falcon automobile to take me the 500 miles to Placerville. I slept in my car and ate what little food I had brought from home. Mr. Bunell was good for his word, and he allowed me 15 minutes to share my heart. I was 25 years old at the time, and one of the missionaries said to me, "Boy, how bad do you want to preach?"

I replied, "Mister, I want to preach."

He said, "Another 200 miles north of here in the top of the Siskew Mountains between California and Oregon, there is a logging camp. They have a small log building that has outdoor toilets and will seat about 80 people. They may come to hear you preach, and they may not. There is a family in the church who will feed you and give you lodging, but I can't promise you that the church people will give you a love offering." Then he added, "Do you still want to go?"

I answered, "You call them and tell them I will be there Saturday night." I cannot tell you the excitement of my heart that God had wonderfully opened the first door as I started back to southern California to get more clothes and to tell Pam and the children that

PRAYER AND FAITH:
The Life of Dr. Tom Williams

I would be going to preach. This same man handed me five dollars at a meal break during this meeting, which was such a blessing to me that evening: I am just over six feet tall, and sleeping in the Falcon for two nights had me feeling somewhat like a pretzel. As I drove through western Nevada returning home, I saw a motel room advertised for five dollars. Knowing Nevada didn't have sales tax, I checked in for a wonderful night of rest! Early the next morning I drove to Newberry, California, where my first wife's brother, who was the pastor of a small church, lived. His parents had told him of my surrender to be an evangelist, so he said, "Tonight is Wednesday night. Why don't you stay and preach for us? The crowd will be small, but it will be an opportunity for you to preach."

I preached that evening and didn't make mention of our financial needs; however, a man who raised chickens for some large poultry corporations did something that night I don't think I shall ever forget. He was about 6 foot 3 inches tall, and as he walked over to me, he looked down at me and said, "Boy, you don't have any money do you?"

"I don't know where you got that information," I said, "but you hit the nail on the head."

He said, "The Lord told me you didn't have any, and I was to give you some." He then put his hand into the side pocket of my suit coat.

I respectfully said, "Whatever amount it is, thank you for listening to the Lord."

I am sure you can imagine that I could hardly wait to get alone so I could see how much he had given me. It was a check for $116! Very honestly, to me it looked like Fort Knox! The next morning I continued driving toward home but made a stop in San Bernardino to visit the home of a couple I had met earlier. I had met this couple one other time when I preached at a youth rally in their church, and I understood from people who knew them well that he prayed several hours a day. I wanted to beseech him to pray for my family and me in the work that God had called us to do. On arriving at their home, I asked him to pray for us. He said he would and that he would put my name at the top of his list. He said, "I believe that God has His hand on your life in a wonderful way."

His wife spoke to him and said, "Are you going to do more for this young man besides pray for him?"

He said, "I was just thinking that God would have us do something for Brother Williams." He opened up his wallet and handed me $100. I proceeded on my way toward home, and when I arrived at the house and handed my wife the $216, she said, "Now, you are an evangelist."

I called a friend of mine who had a small hand-operated printing press and asked him to print 1,000 cards saying I was Evangelist Tom Williams. I also asked him if he would print 100 brochures inviting people to the little church in Oak Run, California, where I would be holding my first meeting. I told my wife and children goodbye, and I was off to that first meeting. I arrived in the little mountain town of Oak Run on Saturday afternoon, and with the help of the family I was to stay with and a few young people, we passed out the brochures I had brought.

We had a fair size group of people on Sunday, and the Lord saved several precious souls that day. By Wednesday night, the little building had standing room only, and we had had 40 people saved in those four days. Many of these were lumberjacks and their families, and a number of them were members of religious movements but had never been truly washed in the blood of the Lamb.

One of the men who hauled logs was in a mill on Thursday at Anderson, California. He told one of the men there what God was doing on the mountain, and this man called his home pastor in Anderson, California, and related what this log hauler had said. The pastor called me Thursday afternoon and asked when I could start preaching in Anderson for him.

I jokingly said, "Pastor, I am booked solid through tomorrow night."

He said, "Start here Sunday morning." The Lord saved 25 people in the morning service that Sunday.

The little church in Oak Run had given me $165, and when I finished in Anderson, they gave me $300. I praise the Lord for what that did for our faith.

The next meeting I had some weeks later was in a small chapel which had been converted from a railroad car. We started the services with only eight people; the Lord blessed, and we had to move to a community building.

Sometimes the meetings I received were weeks apart, but those were great days of building my faith. I had many offers for jobs, but I told them that God had called me to be an evangelist and that He would, by faith, provide.

During these days God sent our second child, Paul, to Pam and me. The Lord had spoken to my heart that He did not want us to have medical or life insurance. I said, "Father, I have done many things for You, but would You speak to Pam's heart also concerning this matter."

Several days later Pam said, "I don't believe the Lord wants us to have insurance."

I said, "He spoke to me about that some time ago, and I asked Him to speak to your heart also."

The insurance agent came to our home and tried to convince us how foolish we were. "You are very wrong about what you are doing," he stated.

I asked him, "How many people smoke every day?"

His answer was, "Millions."

I said, "They are all wrong, not me." I continued. "How many drink every day?"

He again said, "Millions."

I replied, "They are all wrong, not me."

He said, "You say God told you to do this, and you expect me to believe that God talks to you?"

I said, "Not really, because you do not know Jesus Christ as your Saviour." (He belonged to a cult that does not believe there is such a thing as death.) I asked him, "If you do not believe that people really die, then why are you selling life insurance?"

At this point he became very frustrated and told us he would cancel our insurance, and he left. I share all of this to tell you that God miraculously paid the entire bill for Paul's birth. Not only did God provide the needed finances, but He also answered our prayer that Paul would be born before I had to leave for a meeting! The doctors had told me that Paul would not be born for a couple more days, but I needed to leave. I prayed and asked God to allow Paul to be born before I had to leave, and by faith believing God would answer, I told the doctors that Paul would be born before 8:00 a.m. Saturday morning. Paul entered this world at 6:40 a.m. on May 4, 1963, 1 hour and 20 minutes before I had to leave for my meeting!

God provided need after need in answer to prayers of faith. A year after Paul was born, a lawyer friend of mine asked me if Pam had ever adopted Tim. I said, "No, we have not had the money to do that."

He said, "My wife and I would like to take care of all the expenses, and I will handle the legal matter." We proceeded to arrange for the adoption, which is very serious because the biological mother's name is removed from the birth certificate and the adopting mother's name is inserted. We were asked by the judge to bring all of our children on a certain day to meet with him. We dressed them in their Sunday best outfits to make as good an impression on the judge as possible. After the judge had seen the children and talked with all of us, he had no problem with carrying out the adoption. As we walked out of the courtroom, we were very thankful that the Lord had answered our prayer. Someone had given us some money to buy some ice cream to celebrate the adoption, so we stopped at the store and decided that Pam and Tim should be the ones to choose the ice cream flavor since they were the ones involved in the adoption. When we arrived at home, Phyllis walked up to me in her little frilly dress, patent-leather shoes, and holding both her hands on her hips said, "Daddy, when you adopt me, we get to pick the ice cream!" We all had a very good laugh about that.

Approximately two months after I had answered the call to be an evangelist, a pastor of a church in Hemet, California, phoned and asked me to come to be his youth pastor. I told him that I could not come, that I was an evangelist. After a couple more weeks he called a second time to ask me to come to be the youth pastor. I told him that I appreciated very much that he and the church wanted me to come and be on staff, but I again explained that I was an evangelist and could not be his youth pastor. Another two weeks went by, and I received a third phone call from the pastor. Once again I declined to go be the youth pastor.

Around that time following the third phone call from the pastor, I was involved in an automobile accident as I was driving through Stockton, California, on my way to preach in a meeting. The road on which I was traveling was five lanes wide on each side. I was in the far left lane when, for no apparent reason, the car in the far right lane sped across all four lanes, and our two automobiles collided. The impact was so sudden that I went through the windshield of my car. Immediately the Lord spoke to my heart saying, "Are you going to Hemet as youth pastor, or do I have to get tougher?"

The highway patrol arrived on the scene and asked me if I needed to go to the hospital as I had pieces of windshield glass embedded in my head.

I said, "No, Sir, I need to go to a telephone." I called the pastor and told him that God had just spoken to me in a tremendous way, and I would be coming to be his youth pastor. I told him that I would need to continue to preach one meeting a month if God opened the doors. I somehow knew that I would not be staying long with the pastor, and I wanted people to know that I was still an evangelist.

The Lord was taking me to Hemet for two definite reasons: (1) it was Pam's hometown, which would put her near her parents while I traveled, something I had not thought of, but the Lord had; and (2) the young people were in dire need of leadership. Approximately 110 teenagers were in the church, and some adults were spoiling them and trying to win the teenagers' affection. God, in a miraculous way, gave me the hearts of these teenagers and performed a lasting work in their hearts and in their lives.

As I taught them each week, I emphasized that the power of God could be seen through prayer. On one occasion, some of them came to me saying, "We want to see the power of God in prayer that you have been talking about." There were three young men in the church they wanted to see God save, so I asked as many who really wanted that to happen to come to my house on a Saturday night at eight o'clock. Eighteen young people showed up.

Our house was not carpeted, but we knelt on the tiled living room and adjoining dining room floors with two large boxes of Kleenex in the middle. I told them, "The first thing we need to do is get right with each other and then with the Lord because the Bible says in I John 4:20, '*If a man say, I love God, and hateth his brother, he is a liar: for he that loveth not his brother whom he hath seen, how can he love God whom he hath not seen?*' So many Christians try to get their prayers answered, but they have something in their heart against a fellow believer."

The young people began to cross the room and get right with one another. Some young ladies confessed jealousy about another's clothes and looks. Others confessed envy over someone else's popularity. Others confessed gossip and not esteeming others as better than themselves, and many confessed that they had hatred in their heart for one another concerning things that had been done and said. Once this was completed, they then began to tell the Lord how wrong they had been to harbor all of these attitudes in their hearts. This time of confession went on for a couple of hours until everyone's heart was in the right condition to pray for these three young men. They prayed unashamedly, weeping and asking God to save those boys.

The Sunday night following this Saturday night prayer meeting, I told the young people that God would keep His word and save these young men. However, when I finished preaching that Sunday night and gave the invitation, those young men did not come to get saved. The young people came out to the parking lot, surrounded my family and me in our car, and said, "You promised that God would save them tonight," to which I replied, "The night is not over. Let's pray."

While we were praying, a car with these three boys inside turned into the parking lot, pulled alongside my car, and one of them called and asked me to come over.

With trembling voices they said, "Preacher, we have to be saved."

I said, "If you are sincere, get out, and kneel in the headlights of your car in front of all of these young people."

They immediately got out of the car and knelt to receive the Lord Jesus Christ as their Saviour. Those three young men went on to live for the Lord.

When I went back into full-time evangelism, the young people gave me a going-away party which was an experience I have never forgotten. The sight of 110 teenagers standing before me with changed hearts and attitudes was one of the greatest experiences of my ministry. One by one they came with gifts in their hands and tears in their eyes telling me, "Before you came, no one ever loved us enough to get us to do right for God and to teach us the power of prayer. We wanted to give you a gift from each of us so you would remember how much we love and appreciate you." My heart was overflowing that night to think that God would use such a one as I in the lives of those young teens, and I know it reflected upon my face as the tears flowed freely down my cheeks.

It was so exhilarating to watch God move souls to true repentance through the blood of His Son as He did in Santa Susanna, California, at a church of about 150 people, which included about 25 teenagers. The pastor's sons had invited their friends from the public high school with such enthusiasm that many came, including a big fullback from the football team. Now that fullback, whom God saved in the Monday night service, was also enthusiastically inviting his friends to the meetings, and by Wednesday night, we were averaging between 90 and 100 teenagers attending the services.

Each night during the invitation time, this fullback in his earnest naïveté to see his friends saved said to them as he showed them his muscle, "You are getting saved tonight, aren't you?"

With a suppressed smile, I had to say to him each night, "Just invite them to come down the aisle, and let the Holy Spirit work in their heart." Though his method was comical, it was thrilling to see his earnest desire for his friends to receive Christ.

The adults were not to be outdone by the teenagers, and they too were inviting folks to come. One couple invited Roy Rogers and

Dale Evans, and I couldn't believe my eyes that Thursday night when they walked into the church. I was actually seeing my childhood cowboy hero standing in front of me! This couple from the church had become so excited about the moving of the Spirit in the meetings, and their heartfelt invitation was so enticing, that Roy Rogers and his wife decided to come to the church and take part.

I was so impressed when Roy Rogers said to folks as they came to get his autograph, "This is the time to worship the Lord, so I will not be giving out any autographs tonight." As he walked out the door that night, he shook my hand and said, "Young man, if everyone preached like you do, the world would be a different place." That was such an encouragement to me to hear such a compliment from my cowboy hero that I cried in my heart that night, "Oh, Lord, help me to always preach Your Word regardless of who is in the audience."

The power of the Spirit moved upon the community of Santa Susanna that week, and a total of 75 people were brought to the foot of the Cross and met the Saviour there.

The moving of His Holy Spirit went from meeting to meeting, and we experienced another tremendous outpouring while in Perris, California—so much so that people were sitting in the hallways, in the church kitchen, and anywhere else a chair would fit, because the auditorium couldn't seat the crowd! The seed fell upon very fertile soil, and the fruit that came from that meeting was lasting. Sixteen adults became influential workers in the church—two of them being converted from Mormonism. The working God did in that church ignited a flame that continued burning brightly year after year.

The pastor was so thrilled with what God did in that meeting, he invited me back a second time. Once again God shook that community for His glory. The Devil didn't like the loss of his control over that community, and he began to fight back through two very wicked men who angrily voiced their intentions to break up the meeting during one of the services. God, however, had a different plan in mind, and instead of disrupting the service, those two men ran down the aisle, falling on their faces and pleading to be kept alive. They were wonderfully saved.

As a result of God's power coming down in that place, the church attendance grew so steadily a larger building needed to be built to adequately seat everyone. The pastor called to tell me of their situation and asked me to pray that God would give them a larger building. I said, "I'll pray every day for three months if you will ask the church members to pray every day."

During those three months, God reached down and saved a man who was a retired multimillionaire and moved him to Perris just six miles from the church. He began to be a faithful member of the church, and one Sunday he very bluntly said to the pastor, "Your driveway is all dirt. I don't want to drive my Cadillac on dirt. Have the driveway paved and send me the bill."

Pleasantly surprised, the pastor replied, "I agree with you. Thank you, Sir."

Not long after they had the parking lot paved, this same man came to the pastor and said, "This place is much too crowded. What would it cost to build a new auditorium?"

"I'm not sure, but I'll get a quote this week," replied the pastor. The following Sunday, the man handed the pastor an unsigned check for $25,000 and stated, "I will sign the check when the people of the church match this amount."

The pastor excitedly called me and asked, "Would you please pray with us for three weeks? I'm going to take an offering and ask the church people to match this amount."

We both spent the next three weeks on our knees bombarding

Heaven with this request. At the end of that time, we brought the people together to take the special offering. This story occurred in the early 1960s when $25,000 would be like $100,000 today. Some men of the church counted the money after the offering was taken, and we were told the amount totaled a little over $18,000. I leaned over to the pastor and said, "I believe we should take a second offering," and as the men passed the offering plates once more, I prayed for a miracle. The amount from the second offering brought the total to $24,000, but God wasn't finished.

As the pastor announced to the people the amount received, a little boy in the congregation on the pastor's left stood up, and speaking with a lisp, he said, "Pastor, I have $8.00 in my piggy bank, and my mom and dad told me I could give it."

Another small child stood up in the back and said, "I have about $20.00 in savings, and my parents told me I could give it."

This went on for several minutes with different children offering all they had when from the very back of the church a couple with tears freely flowing said, "We have $2,000 saved for a trip to the Bahamas because we never had a honeymoon, but the church needs a building more than we need to go to the Bahamas."

The men jubilantly shouted that the amount had come to a total of just over $27,000, and the retired multimillionaire walked to the front of the auditorium and signed his check. He turned to the pastor and said, "Build it, Brother, and I will pay the rest of the entire amount." What a wonderful experience to learn and have been a part of in my early years! There really is a God in Heaven Who answers the prayer of faith!

Out of this same church in Perris, California, God worked a miracle for me and my family. Being apart from my family so much was very difficult for all of us, so we began asking the Lord for a travel trailer so we could at least be together in the summer. We had traveled one summer together in our car and cooked our meals on the tailgate using a small Coleman stove. We knew it wasn't the best way to travel with the family, so by faith we had a hitch installed on our car to be ready for God's answer.

His answer came one day when a man out of the church in Perris called and said, "There is a beautiful travel trailer for sale close by your house. I want to go to the bank with you and cosign the note so you can buy it." When I hung up, we whooped and hollered our elation, and I left to meet the man at the bank. When we sat down to talk with the president of the bank, he swore using God's name in a tremendously profane way for no obvious reason.

I immediately rebuked the president of the bank, then turned to my friend, and said, "Let's go, I don't want to borrow money from a man who thinks so little of my Saviour." I knew this stand meant we would not get the trailer, and Pam's heart would be as broken as mine was, but I had to stand up for my Lord.

By the time I drove the 20 miles to our house, I was singing and praising God for giving me the courage to do what I had done at the bank. When I came in so happy, Pam said with a great amount of enthusiasm, "You got the trailer!"

I told her, "No, Sweetheart, I did not get the trailer, but let me tell you what happened." As I repeated the story to her, her emotions were very mixed. She was elated that I had spoken up for our Saviour, but so broken that she and the children would not be going. Suddenly the phone rang, and this same friend who offered to cosign with me was on the other end in tears. "Tom, you did today to the banker what I should have done years ago. I am ashamed that I have let him curse my Saviour for years and never spoke up. Please come get the trailer; I just paid for it." God wonderfully answered prayer again with our need for a way to travel together being met just three days before my summer preaching schedule began. I have found in my years of serving God that if I will stand for Him, He will honor me.

In the first five years of our ministry, the Lord taught me to wait upon Him in prayer and faith as He was miraculously building a man only He knew would face greater trials and greater victories in the years to come. Our finances were a constant struggle; many times we didn't have any money, like the time the car payment, the rent payment, and the gas payment were all overdue. We heard the bank was threatening to repossess our car, the gas company was threatening to turn off the gas, and the landlord was threatening to turn us out. I knew God had to get involved, and He had to intervene soon. One night after Pam and the children were in bed, I got down on my knees before the Lord and didn't get up until the answer came. At 3:00 a.m. I heard a knock at the front door. When I answered the door, I saw on our front porch a silver-haired man who attended our church. His face was as white as a sheet, and his hands clutched tightly to hundreds of dollars. He said, "God told me three days ago to bring you this money, but I wouldn't. I don't want to give you this money now, but I haven't been able to sleep, and I MUST get some rest. So here, take the money." That money was the exact amount we needed, and it paid every outstanding bill we owed. The Bible says God will make men to give into your hands, and He certainly did that for us. It was a joy in the years following to become very good friends with that good man; he often drove many miles to hear me preach. From time to time, God used him to meet financial needs of our ministry.

Another miracle God wrought to build my faith in His ability to provide centered again on the fact that we did not have any money. Our cupboards were bare, little was in the refrigerator when the Lord spoke to my heart and told me to go grocery shopping. I told Pam what the Lord had said to me, and she said, "Honey, we don't have any money."

I answered, "I know; that's what I told the Lord, but He told me that He didn't ask me if I had any money, just to go shopping." I got the family in the car and drove down the main street of our town. I said, "Father, there are three supermarkets in this town. Which one do you want me to go to?" I was driving toward the Alpha Beta Grocery Store, and the Lord told me to turn in and shop at that market.

When we got into the store, I told Pam to stack as much in the basket as she possibly could because, "It doesn't take any more faith to pay for a full basket than it does for half a basket when you do not have any money." She did such a great job of loading the basket that by the time we wound up at the meat market she had to stuff hamburger in every crack that was left. Once we were finished filling our shopping cart, I told Pam to start for the checkout stand, and she said to me, "You start for the checkout stand." Heading for the nearest checkout station, I began to roll the basket up the aisle toward the cash registers when a very nicely dressed lady stepped in front of our basket and said, "Sir, God just told me to pay for everything in your basket." At that point, and as I write this book, I can only say, "Hallelujah, what a God we serve!"

God once again showed His power to provide as I was leaving a meeting in Tacoma, Washington, and traveled on my way home to Southern California. I only had $1.68, and the Lord asked me, "Tom, can you drive 1,200 miles on a $1.68 worth of gas?"

I replied, "If You tell me I can, then, yes, I can."

His next words to me were, "Let's go," and I started toward home. I had some gas in the tank and drove till it ran out. I pulled

PRAYER AND FAITH:
The Life of Dr. Tom Williams

into a gas station and told the attendant that I had $1.68 and no more because in those days gas stations weren't self serve.

Shortly after I asked him to give me only $1.68 worth of gas, the Lord sent a covey of cars to that station. The service station attendant was frantically running from car to car, filling their tanks. He had not shut off my pump, but he had left the nozzle in my car and filled my tank. When he came back, he said, "That's okay, Sir. It's my mistake." That tank of gas took me into northern California along what was known as Highway 99. I was passing through a small city and stopped for a red light when I heard someone call my name. I looked to my left and saw a man I had met the year before while I had been preaching in the church he attended. He motioned for me to pull over to the curb, which I did. He walked over to my car and said, "When I saw you just now, the Lord laid on my heart to buy you a tank of gas." We drove to a gas station; he filled my car with gas, then turned and asked me, "Are you as hungry as your car?"

I told him, "I really am." We left the gas station and drove to a restaurant where he bought me a wonderful lunch before I started on my way toward home again. God miraculously provided for my gas all the rest of the way home, and I pulled into my driveway having only spent $1.68 on gas.

There have been times when I didn't have any money for plane tickets, but by faith went to the airport believing God would provide. The day I was to fly to Kansas from Los Angeles, the Lord told me to go to the airport and fly even though I had no money. I was standing in line to purchase my ticket when I heard my name paged over the loudspeaker telling me to go to the nearest phone. As I picked up the receiver, Pam was on the other end, and she said, "I thought you might like to know that a man called here for your flight information. He called the counter in L.A., and your ticket has been paid." God is so faithful that I have no way to explain Him to you until you also have believed Him.

∽

One of the great trials of my faith during these early years was a return trip home from visiting family and preaching in Texas. We lacked about 35 miles from finishing a 2,500-mile round trip when I ran into the back of a semi-truck loaded with 80,000 pounds, and I was driving the 70 miles per hour speed limit. I cannot tell you why I did not see the truck. I know that some people call it road hypnosis, but whatever it was, it caused me to think that the truck was moving faster than it was.

Our son Tim was in the back seat of the car playing a game of stacking pillows on Phyllis, who was four. When I hit the truck, Tim was thrown from the back seat into the back of the front passenger's seat. As a result, the passenger seat came down and threw Pam head first into the dash of the car. Tim was catapulted into the windshield just below where it fastens to the top of the car. The windshield should have shattered, which would have propelled Tim into the back of the semi-truck. Instead, the windshield bubbled out six inches, keeping Tim inside the car. Tim wore glasses; at the point of impact, the lenses of his glasses were left lying side by side down on the dash while the frames remained on his face.

When I came to, four of my front teeth were gone from the tremendous impact of my head's hitting the steering wheel. In those days the seat belt only came across the waist. I don't know if I saw the truck just before I hit it, because I gripped the steering wheel so hard that I bent it down around the steering column on both sides. The engine of the car was lying on the dashboard. The truck had two steel bars close together down the back of it for backing up to loading docks. If it had not been for the 2 bars, we would have gone under the truck.

I was bleeding from my mouth and from a chest laceration. Tim was bleeding from a head injury; with every heartbeat, blood was shooting across the car. I did not know what to do, so I ripped off my shirt and tried to put it in the hole in his head. I remember looking up toward Heaven and crying, "Oh God, help us."

At that point I did not know whether or not Pam and our two-year-old son, Paul, were dead. Paul had been in the front seat with us, and his little body had been thrown down against the floorboard. I was to find out later how thankful I would become for hair rollers. Pam had put up her hair while we were traveling because we were going to a watch night service as soon as we arrived home. She had large wire rollers in her hair, and as she went into the dash, her head was turned sideways. The rollers cushioned the impact as they were flattened from a two-inch diameter to tissue-paper thickness. Because they had taken much of the beating, Pam's life was saved. The truck driver could do nothing about helping us get to a hospital. I was wondering how we would get to the hospital when a man and his family pulled up in their car. I told the man, "I know we'll ruin your car, but if you'll help us, I will buy you another car."

He said, "My car is full," and drove off to leave my family to die.

Thank God for the next car that stopped and the man who said, "Put your family in here and let me get you to the hospital." When I moved Pam and the children into the car, there wasn't any room for me. I said, "Take my family to the hospital in Banning, California, and I will be there shortly." The very next car that stopped was a man in a Corvette. I quickly related to him what had happened. He said, "Sir, I work at that hospital. Get in for the ride of your life."

I am not sure how fast he drove, but it must have been well over 100 miles per hour. My family had just been put into the emergency room, and their first concern was for Tim who was in a state of shock. Because of his condition, anesthesia could not be administered. Therefore, the emergency room personnel had rolled him up inside of many sheets until he was unable to move and began to work on his head to stop the bleeding.

One of the hardest things of my life was when he started yelling, "Daddy, they're killing me! Daddy, they're killing me! Help me!" Of course, I could do nothing for him, so I cried out to God for His help.

In the midst of all this trauma, something humorous happened. The family had spent some time in Texas with one of my brothers whose nickname is "Bear." He was a very big and very strong man, and my son Tim admired and loved his Uncle Bear. When I would not help him, he told the doctors, "If my Uncle Bear was here, he would take care of you guys." After about two and a half hours, the doctors had us stabilized, and we were sent by ambulance to a hospital closer to our home. Pam was not dead, but she was in severe shock and did not recognize any of us for the next five days. Paul's left eyelid was cut open, and he had some internal bleeding. Phyllis was not hurt at all; she had simply rolled onto the back floorboard on top of all the pillows that she and Tim had been playing with. I was all right except for some internal bleeding and a severely painful mouth. The doctors were trying to get me into a hospital bed, but I was so concerned about the family that I refused until early the next morning. Four times that night the doctors called for an ambulance to rush Tim to San Bernardino, California, to a larger hospital because of brain swelling. Four times the doctors cancelled the ambulance. Each time for some unknown reason, the swelling would decrease. Early the next morning I was to learn why. My pastor and the pastor from the church in Perris walked into my room at the same time and said, "Tom, both of our churches were having a watchnight service, and we never went home all night. Our churches prayed all night long for your family." I knew that once again our God had so wonderfully provided our needs.

Faith simply believes God—that He will do as He has promised. He tells us in His Word that He will clothe us, He will feed us, He will answer when we call, and that He will do abundantly above what we could ask or think. In Hebrews 11:6 He tells us, *"But without faith it is impossible to please him: for he that cometh to God must believe that he is, and that he is a rewarder of them that diligently seek him."* It doesn't say that it is probable; it says it is IMPOSSIBLE to please Him without faith. God is just waiting for someone to believe Him; and when a person does, it encourages his heart and glorifies God's name. These lessons I learned in my early years of ministry have been tremendously valuable to me as I continue to walk with the Lord each day.

CHAPTER FOUR

⁓⁓

The Next Step of Faith

THE YEARS IN HEMET, CALIFORNIA, were mightily blessed of God, and He built a foundation for our ministry on the West Coast. One of the many blessings was the birth of our third child, Penny, born March 10, 1967. Pam really didn't want any more children after our son Paul was born, but our Heavenly Father in His mercy was answering a prayer that Pam had prayed earlier in our marriage. Pam was a brunette, and Phyllis was a blond. Pam prayed that she would have a little girl who looked just like her. Penny was an exact duplicate of her mother, not only in looks, but also in personality and in every other characteristic. The misgivings that Pam had during the pregnancy were all turned to joy when she saw our new little daughter.

The Lord brought about many circumstances which facilitated our moving to Denver, Colorado, in 1967. One circumstance involved our children and the Christian school in Hemet. Our son Tim was entering the seventh grade, and the Christian school in Hemet only went up to the sixth grade. As a result, Tim began his seventh grade year in the public school, and it did not take long for me to know I did not want him to remain in the public school system. Very few Christian schools went through the twelfth grade anywhere in America in 1967; however, one of the very best was located in Denver, Colorado. My ministry was also growing, and I needed to be more centrally located, so we put our home up for sale in the autumn of 1967. The Lord blessed, as our house immediately sold, and we began our move to Colorado. That move to Colorado would be a trip never to be forgotten.

We hired a moving company to move our furniture to Colorado while we followed, pulling our 24-foot travel trailer behind our car. We were at the city limits of Hemet when the wiring harness between the car and trailer completely burned up, delaying us several hours while having it fixed. Once we were able to get back on the road, we headed toward Prescott, Arizona, to see Pam's sister. A few miles out of Prescott, the alternator went out on the car. It would take us two days to get that fixed. Exhausted from all the driving, we finally arrived in Gallup, New Mexico, late in the evening on Saturday. I asked Pam for the keys to the trailer, and as she was searching through her purse, she suddenly looked up and said, "Oh no, Honey. I left them on the counter at the trading post where we stopped today."

For years I have preached that reaction is as important or maybe more important than action. This was a time for the correct reaction, which I probably did not give at that late hour. I began to take off the compartment door from the back of the trailer. After removing about 25 screws, I was able to crawl up inside and push the couch out of the way in order to get into the trailer and open the door. This procedure took about two hours, and we praised the Lord all the children had fallen asleep.

We wanted to get up the next morning and get to Albuquerque, New Mexico, so we left Gallup at six in the morning. About one mile later, we heard a loud noise. I stopped to investigate and discovered that a bolt had fallen out of the spring of one side of the trailer, causing the trailer to rest on the two tires that were on that side. I prayed and started walking back to Gallup in hopes of finding the bolt that had come out. I miraculously found it, but now I needed the nut to screw onto the bolt. Nothing was open that time of morning; however, I noticed a junkyard located close by the city limits sign. When I finally was able to awaken the owner of the junkyard, I told him my problem, and he sleepily said, "If you can find a nut, it's yours." While he went back to bed, I started my search, which lasted about an hour. When it looked like my search was futile, in His mercy the Lord opened my eyes, and I found one.

I returned to the trailer, jacked it up, and fixed the problem. We were once again on our way. By the time we reached Albuquerque, it was too late to attend church, so we continued on toward Santa Fe, New Mexico. Halfway between Albuquerque and Santa Fe, we heard another loud noise. I pulled over to the side of the road, and to my dismay, two tires on the trailer had blown out at the same time. I had to unhitch the trailer and drive 50 miles one way to find a tire to fit, as I only had one spare. After a loss of about four hours, we continued on.

After all our mishaps, we reached Denver, Colorado; however, we learned the moving van, which should have arrived three days ahead of us, had broken down in New Mexico. While going through these types of situations when following the leading of the Lord, **absolutely** knowing you are in the will of God strengthens your faith.

This reminds me of Matthew, chapter 14, where the Lord Jesus tells His apostles to get in the ship and go to the other side of the Sea of Galilee. They were doing exactly **what** He told them, **when** He told them, **where** He told them; yet they found themselves in a storm. Being in a storm does not mean that you are out of the will of God. What you need to do is keep your eye not on the storm, but on the God of the storm. The moving van finally arrived, and we settled in our new home in a suburb of Denver called Littleton. We immediately enrolled our children in the Christian school, which they loved and in which they did very well.

PRAYER AND FAITH:
The Life of Dr. Tom Williams

❧❧

I had always had a burden to have a ranch where people could come and enjoy preaching in a western, cowboy-type atmosphere. We had been in Denver almost one year when, on one of my trips east to preach, I met an individual who gave me the money for a down payment on a ranch. I knew of a beautiful ranch called the Singing River Ranch in the mountains west of Evergreen, Colorado, and it was owned by a group of churches who needed to sell it. Its many facilities, such as cabins, dormitories, a dining room, a lodge, and a 400-seat chapel, made it ideal for guests. A 40-foot-wide mountain stream that was fed from a glacier on Mount Evans ran directly through the ranch. The ranch was home to elk, deer, and many other kinds of wildlife.

My family and I took the greatest step of faith in moving there to operate it for the Lord, and He rewarded our faith. We saw a great number of people saved at the ranch as well as tremendous decisions made in the lives of Christians.

While we lived on the ranch, the Lord sent many tremendous trials which tested and stretched our faith as never before. We had now moved from just providing for our family monthly to providing for the three families the Lord had provided to help us run the ranch, plus the ranch payment itself. During the summer, the additional salaries for summer staff added to our financial responsibilities, and the utilities for the ranch were overwhelming compared to what we were used to paying just for a home. Our Heavenly Father was shaping us for a time that we had no idea would come. The ranch was used of God to drive us further upon our knees, often hours at a time.

One summer night I was praying all night in the office, and unbeknownst to me, one of the young staff men could not sleep that night. He saw the light on in the office; and walking toward the office, he could hear me praying the closer he came. This young man leaned against the wall outside the office all night long and listened to me pray. It was many years later before I would know about this incident.

In the 1980s I was preaching a revival meeting where this same gentleman was in attendance, and he was asked to give a testimony of how he came to start a camp of his own. He told how he came to work at Singing River Ranch one summer, and his opening statement was, "Brother Williams took me on a trial basis. I didn't even know which end of the horse to bridle." He then told of the night he couldn't sleep and how he listened to me pray, ending his story by saying, "When I heard Brother Williams pray all night long, it changed my life." This man started a camp by learning as a young man at Singing River Ranch to have a life of prayer.

There were many times when Pam and I worked 18 to 20 hours a day. We would have needed at least another full-time family and probably ten more summer staff to relieve the heavy work load and the long hours we had to keep. I do not know what I would have done without her help. We were both walking where we had never walked financially, emotionally, or physically.

Something funny happened on one of those nights when we worked till 2:00 in the morning. Along with Pam's many other jobs, she was also the bookkeeper. We were sitting in the office, and she was trying to find where our books were wrong by 16¢. I did not know what she was looking for, and I know very little about bookkeeping, so I said, "What is so important, and what are you looking for?"

She said, "Somewhere the books are off by 16¢." When I handed her a quarter and said, "Let's go to bed," she said, "You can't do that. If we juggle the books for 16¢, it would be like doing it for thousands of dollars. We have to account for every penny." Even though it was funny, it was one of the greatest lessons I have ever learned. I looked at her and said, "The Bible says that we must all give an account." All of a sudden I found I wasn't sleepy or exhausted anymore as I realized that God's bookkeeping was far superior to ours.

Though there were many trials and burdens at Singing River Ranch, there were certainly some great blessings and times of tremendous joy. We were able to build a large rodeo arena, and a number of horses were donated to the ranch. The Lord in His goodness had given me back my cowboy image and allowed me to live in a place more wonderful than I could have dreamed. Some of the great times were in the early morning hours when I would go down and break some of the young horses.

A funny incident occurred one day when a lady called from Colorado Springs, Colorado, and said she had a pretty black horse she would like to give to the ranch. I took two men with me who were fairly good cowboys because she said the horse was running loose on 1,500 acres of land. When we arrived at her ranch, I told one of the men with me to ride in one direction while the other man and I rode in the opposite direction. I wanted to try to get the horse in a corner where we could rope him. He rode off in the direction I told him and was gone about 20 minutes when he came galloping over a hill shouting, "I caught him, I caught him!" I couldn't believe what I was hearing because it is very difficult to corner a horse by yourself, and it is very hard for a horse carrying a rider to chase down a horse that is running free. I asked, "Did you really catch him?"

He said, "Boss, I've got my rope around him." We rode about a mile, and sure enough he had roped the horse quite easily. For reasons unknown, the horse had been dead about two days. He had cleverly put his rope around the dead horse's head and came with his wonderful story. We called the lady who had donated the horse and told her the situation. She apologized, saying, "I have not been out there for about a week to check on the horse."

Many additional funny situations happened at the ranch concerning horses. When people would come out to ride, we, of course, would ask them how experienced they were so we could put them on a horse that they could enjoy. I remember one teenage girl who told us she rode all the time. I gave her a nice little horse named Apache. I held the reins until she sat down in the saddle, then handed them to her, and stepped back. She screamed, dropped the reins on Apache's neck, and grabbed the saddle horn with both hands. Apache immediately took off running.

I jumped on my horse and started chasing them. By the time I caught up with them, the young lady had fallen off and was injured. I said to her, "You have never ridden a horse."

She explained while sobbing in pain from a broken collarbone, "I have watched it a lot on television."

One day the welfare department brought 12 young boys to the ranch to ride horses. As they trotted the horses up and down the arena, they called to one another saying, "I'm Roy Rogers!" or "I'm Gene Autry!" or "I'm John Wayne!" It did my heart good to see them having so much fun.

One of the boys pulled too hard on the reins of his horse, and the horse reared up just a little bit. The boy called out to me, "My horse popped a wheelie!"

It was a great time, and when the boys were finished riding, I was then able to tell them why the ranch was there and about the goodness of the Lord. I told them how Jesus Christ had saved me, and all 12 of them received the Lord Jesus as their Saviour. It is wonderful how God can use us in a marvelous way to win others to our Saviour!

I remember the time a bus load of young people from Chicago came to the ranch for a week. The altitude at the ranch was 7,200 feet high, and we constantly had to remind people the air was harder to breathe at that altitude—especially during an activity. Because many of these young people had never been to a mountainous area, they did not believe it would be harder to breathe. The mountain behind the lodge went up to nearly 9,000 feet, and one day during their stay, the young people began to run up the side of that mountain. They ran only 100 yards before they had to sit down to catch their breath. Breathing loud and hard, they finally agreed it was indeed harder to breathe in higher altitudes!

At their request, the next day I took them on a hike up the side of that 9,000-foot mountain. From there they could see Mount Evans which was several miles to the west of the ranch and only visible from the top of this mountain. Mount Evans was beautifully snow-capped when these young people were visiting, and what happened that day was something I will remember as long as I live. As we approached the top and Mount Evans came into view, all 40 of those young people began to sing, as if they had been directed, the wonderful hymn, "How Great Thou Art." As I write this book nearly 40 years later, I weep at the memory of such an exhilarating time. I am sure that Heaven rejoiced that day.

Many were helped at Singing River Ranch, but for some reason, God did not allow me to keep the ranch beyond three years. It was a severe test of my faith to move off of this beautiful place and keep going for the Lord. I am so thankful that John Newton wrote the song "Amazing Grace" because the third verse says, "And grace will lead me home." Indeed, His amazing grace does carry us on.

I am sure some will ask if the ranch was the will of God. Some will say, "If it was His will, then why didn't He let you keep it?" I cannot give you a complete answer because His ways are past finding out. I just know for my life and for the life of my family, Singing River Ranch was a stepping stone to higher ground. The Lord used it to give me back my cowboy image, which only Heaven will reveal how God has used it all of these years following Singing River.

CHAPTER FIVE

༄

The Door That Faith Opened

FOLLOWING OUR RESPITE AT SINGING River Ranch, we moved to Pine, Colorado, which was a small town still in the mountains but several miles south. We lived there for only a year before God moved us to a suburb of Denver, which put us closer to the Christian school our children attended. Soon after returning to the Denver area, a number of circumstances were directed by the Lord which led my family and me to begin attending South Sheridan Baptist Church. At this church the Lord enabled me to meet Dr. Jack Hudson, the pastor of Northside Baptist Church of Charlotte, North Carolina. Dr. Hudson and I were both preaching at the Bible conference being held by South Sheridan Baptist Church when the Lord united our hearts, and we were to become great friends for years to come. Through my meeting Dr. Hudson, the Lord opened a door that would catapult our ministry into greater heights.

༄

The Southwide Baptist Fellowship met in several different churches in those years, and when their meetings were held at Northside Baptist Church in the early 1970s, Dr. Hudson was appointed as the moderator for the meeting. At the last moment Dr. Lee Roberson developed a voice problem, and Dr. Hudson asked me to come and preach in his place. I could not believe what the Lord was doing in affording me the opportunity to speak to hundreds of pastors at one time, and it was with fear and trepidation coupled with large doses of humility that I accepted the invitation. I could not preach in Dr. Roberson's place, but I knew God could take this little country boy now from Colorado and use him as a vessel for His glory if He so desired. I have to believe that the Lord did this because by faith my family and I went on after losing Singing River Ranch. I was actually preaching another meeting during this time, so I asked the pastor to give me one day off in order to preach at Southwide. I purchased a plane ticket to Charlotte and landed at the airport late at night. The next morning I walked to the restaurant near the motel and found the restaurant to be full of preachers. My cowboy hat, boots, and Western suit drew quite a bit of attention as I walked into the restaurant. As they were noticing me, I noticed only one chair was available, at a table where three pastors were sitting. I asked the three men if I could sit and eat breakfast with them, and they kindly invited me to have a chair. One of them asked, "Are you the cowboy preacher who is speaking this morning?"

I said, "Yes, I am."

He then said, "You really must be something after the build up Dr. Hudson gave you last night." This statement really added to my anxiety about preaching in the absence of Dr. Roberson, and I was ever so thankful that God had put on my heart to preach a message titled "Is Anything Too Hard for the Lord?" Knowing that nothing was too hard for the Lord and knowing that it would be the Lord working through me helped me to walk to the pulpit that morning to preach. I cannot begin to tell you how the Lord took that message and used it so mightily that morning.

A few weeks later Dr. Hudson and a pastor who had been at the fellowship meeting went fishing, and they were not having any success catching fish. This pastor said to Dr. Hudson, "Do you remember that message 'Is Anything Too Hard for the Lord?' Brother Tom Williams preached at Southwide?"

Dr. Hudson said, "Yes, I remember."

This pastor then said, "Let's ask God to help us catch fish." They prayed, and in the next two hours they caught an unbelievable number of fish. Dr. Hudson told that story over and over at places where he would preach. From time to time, many other pastors whom I saw later on would say to me, "I'll never forget that message, 'Is Anything Too Hard for the Lord?'" I rejoice that God's Word is so effective and powerful.

Our ministry began to blossom like a flower opening up on a beautiful, sunny morning. Pastors from across the country began to call and write asking me to come and hold evangelistic meetings at their churches. The number of calls I was receiving was astounding, and I could not begin to accept all of the invitations that were extended my way. Our ministry now began to cover all 50 states rather than just the West Coast and a smattering of eastern and central states. Some of the literally hundreds and hundreds of independent Baptist churches in the South began opening their doors to me and my ministry. Not only was I hearing from more churches, I was receiving invitations to preach at various statewide conferences and at Bible colleges across the nation. Prior to this wonderful opportunity, I occasionally took a song leader and soloist to meetings with me; however, now I felt our ministry needed a full-time music man as we were going into larger churches and to area-wide campaigns.

At this same time, God led me to take my family with me full-time, so in the spring of 1975 we put our home up for sale and purchased a 35-foot motor home. That was a very difficult time for all of us in letting go of many precious items which had been a part of our family for years. Each one of us down to the smallest child experienced some real battles with letting go of things which had become very precious.

I think for Pam it was mainly some of the furniture items, such

as a china cabinet with special memories attached. When I had traveled by myself, churches often gave me a certain amount of money
to pay for my meals while I was there. I began to fast and save that
designated money so I could take Pam to choose her dream china
cabinet. After several months of saving, I finally had the amount I
needed and took her shopping for the cabinet. She was so surprised
and overwhelmed and, of course, wondered how I had gotten all the
money. When I told her I had fasted and saved the money for the
cabinet, it became a very cherished item to her.

Our children were all great readers, and I think for them as far
as material possessions, their books were probably the hardest things
to leave behind. It may seem odd to some, but for our smaller children, the precious things were some of their special toys that they
loved to play with. Then, of course, friends and schoolmates ranked
very high in what they would miss.

For me it was a tremendous time of soul searching. I owned a
library of 2,500 books that I had collected and had been given as
gifts over the years. I called the preachers in the Denver area and
arranged a time when they could come over and purchase the books
at giveaway prices. I suppose if I had to do that part again, I would
have listened to my pastor, Dr. Ed Nelson, who begged me not to sell
my library. He offered to store it for me until later on in life when I
might have another home.

In my zeal and determination to burn all the bridges, I probably
did a real injustice to my family. I know I was in the will of God in
taking them with me, but I probably could have been more lenient
in some of the things that I severed. I just so wanted to please God
and do what I could for Him that I knew no other way to say to Him
I was willing to sell out for Him. I so often think of Calvary when my
Saviour Who was facing the greatest hours of His earthly stay cried
out, "...*not my will, but thine....*"

CHAPTER FIVE
The Door That Faith Opened

Being all together as a family was a blessing to us as well as a blessing to the churches because the people could see our family together and be encouraged to hold family altars in their own homes as well as spend time together as a family unit. I appreciated Pam's effort to homeschool the children and to make the most of a continual life in a motor home. She was, outside of God, the greatest part of my ministry. In many ways there were trials that we had to work through, and we praised God for His grace and mercy.

Once we started on the road full-time, we took another giant step of faith and purchased two other motor homes for the two families that we had hired, the Grinsteads and the Criswells. We hired Brother Grinstead to be our music man and Brother Criswell to follow the Southeastern Rodeo Association (S.R.A.) of which I was chaplain. We met Brother Bud Grinstead and his wife Sherry and their three children, Debbie, Darryl, and Dawn in Alabama. Brother Bud was the music director for a church in Alabama when I approached him with the offer of joining our team and traveling full-time. Following a number of weeks of prayer, they, by the leading of the Lord, joined our team.

We met Brother Bob Criswell, his wife Ethel and their children, Cheryl, Colleen, and Clinton in New York. Brother Bob was an evangelist as well as a cowboy who performed rope tricks and owned a horse named Cloudy that also performed tricks. I had an overwhelming burden to reach cowboys for Christ, and this was the family God directed me to hire to represent God through our ministry in reaching cowboys for Christ. Bob also played a guitar, and their family sang together, which was an added attraction to the cowboy church services.

We wanted to protect our families from the overexhaustion of being in meetings week after week and night after night. Bud and I, of course, went to the meetings each night, where he sang the solos and I preached. However, our wives and children alternated coming to the meetings every other night; they sang the nights they attended.

Each weekend the Criswells were in a different city as they followed the rodeos, and on Wednesday nights Brother Bob preached in a church somewhere on the way to the next rodeo town. The rodeo services were held usually in the rodeo arenas or at a barn somewhere on the rodeo grounds. This proved to be a very successful ministry that the Lord blessed in an unusual way. A great number of souls were saved including a number of the S.R.A. champion cowboys and cowgirls. Other rodeo associations began asking us to come and speak. The S.R.A. finals were always held at the coliseum in Charlotte, North Carolina.

The recognition that we gained from this led to my being asked to speak at the Mountain Rodeo Association Finals which were held at the coliseum in Bismarck, North Dakota. Through a series of situations in the rodeo world, I was asked to come and speak at the National High School Finals Rodeo, which that year was held in Sulfur Spring, Louisiana. We had written a tract specifically for the cowboys called, "Holy Horses." We wanted to draw their attention to the fact horses are mentioned more than 200 times in the Bible.

During this rodeo we passed out 10,000 of those tracts one night as I carried the Christian flag into the arena on horseback. The announcer told the crowd of more than 10,000 people why I was there and why I was carrying the Christian flag. He also said that night, "Ladies and gentlemen, all of my life I have heard of 'holy cow,' but never 'holy horses.'"

One night during this rodeo a gentleman walked up to me and said, "It is really unique what you are doing. My name is Peter Jenkins, and I am doing a unique thing by walking across America." I had no way of knowing that sometime later he would write a book by that title which would be very popular. I was glad that I had an opportunity to share Christ with him.

During this same time, God began to publicize our ministry when a couple of national magazines wrote an article on the work we were doing with the rodeos. Some major television networks also interviewed me concerning the rodeo ministry. It was so wonderful to see how God was using us to proclaim the name of Christ, and we counted ourselves to be very blessed.

It wasn't long until we realized that 35-foot motor homes with their limited storage were not conducive to our full-time traveling needs. I began to pray that the Lord would help us to buy something larger. In my search for what would be the very best, God led me to purchase three used Silver Eagle Continental Trailway buses. In talking to a number of people who had purchased buses from this company, I was told it was impossible to bargain with the man in charge of sales. I have always been one who never wanted to pay someone's asking price, so I prayed much that the Lord would go before me. I also knew that cash talks.

The day that I went to purchase the buses, I took two things with me—a top-rate mechanic and a briefcase full of cash. We found three buses that we felt were the best they had, and I made an offer for all three which the man turned down. I opened the briefcase and said, "You wouldn't want this much cash to walk out of here would you?"

He said, "I don't believe I or the company would, so you just bought three buses." I praise the Lord that He had worked another miracle which saved us thousands of dollars. Two men in the Dallas area joined with me to drive them to Birmingham, Alabama, where they would be converted into Class A motor homes. We would have more room inside in addition to all of the tremendous storage area beneath, plus the big diesel engines would give us more power, better

mileage, and longer engine life. The buses proved to be a great blessing to the team.

∽∾

We had some wonderful meetings and great times of fellowship
with the Grinstead family while we traveled together. One of those
meetings took place in Parsippany, New Jersey, at the Parsippany
Baptist Church. We had gone there for a week-long meeting, and
right from the very start the Holy Spirit was moving in a tremendous
way. I do not recall how many, but we saw a great number saved, and
the Christians were brought very close to the heart of God. The
crowds kept growing until we didn't even have standing room, and
people were standing outside the building at every entrance. There
wasn't one square foot of space that wasn't filled with people. They
were even sitting all across the platform, which kept me from walking around like I usually do while I preach.

During the closing night, I told the people if they wanted to get
saved that they would need to get up and go outside because there
wasn't any room to come forward. A number of people did go outside and met with personal workers and were gloriously saved.
Meetings such as this one where we experienced God's great power
and ability to move people's hearts unto Himself made the many
hours of travel and sacrifices all worth it.

∽∾

While we were holding revival meetings at the First Baptist
Church in North Tonawanda, New York, we were experiencing a
tremendous outpouring of God's presence, and many souls were
coming to the Saviour. One day during this meeting the pastor and
I went to the hospital to call on a woman whom he had been seeking to win to the Saviour. However, this lady continually told him
that her cigarettes were her god. When we arrived at the hospital
and reached her room, she said to us with a barely audible voice,

"Your God has defeated my god: I have cancer of the throat and lungs, and I need to be saved and baptized." She received Christ there in the hospital, and when she was released from the hospital, she was gloriously baptized at the church by the pastor while I held a handkerchief over her tracheotomy. Needless to say, the Lord used this incident to stir the whole church as she told the church what she had told the pastor and me.

Another lady in this same church had tried for years to get her husband, who was a devout evolutionist and the head of the philosophy department at the University of Buffalo, to come to church with her. One night during these meetings he finally agreed to attend with her. I was aware that he was coming, so I spent much time praying about what to preach. I knew God was directing me to preach a message titled, "The Bible *vs.* Evolution." The entire message upset her husband, and as he and his wife walked out the building that night, he didn't have any interest in speaking to me or in shaking my hand.

The next morning his wife called the church in tears and asked to speak to me. She said, "Brother Williams, I do not understand. I have worked all these years to get my husband to church, and then you purposely preached against what he believed."

I assured her that I had spent much time in prayer about what God would have me to preach, and that I would continue to pray for her husband's salvation. Two nights later I was so thankful to God and so thrilled when I saw him come into the building for the service. When I gave the invitation, he came forward and said, "I have hardly slept since I was here the other night. You made what I believed and taught for so many years look so ridiculous that for the first time in my life I really saw what I was teaching. I want to be saved and live my life for the God Who created all that there is." I cannot tell you the joy that filled his wife's heart and how thankful she was that I had listened to the leading of the Lord concerning what to preach. Faith does not try to understand God; faith just believes Him.

∽෨෮

Even with the evangelistic team and the tremendous expense of the three coaches, we never established that a church had to have so many people or be able to give a certain offering for us to come. A small church in Illinois had asked us if we would come to a church with an attendance of only 60 people. The pastor said, "With fear and trembling in my heart, I am inviting you to come for a Sunday through Friday meeting." I assured him that we did not require that a church be so big or do so much for us.

We took the team and drew quite a bit of attention in this small farming community with our two big coaches and our two families. Right from the start, the Lord began to move in the church, in the town, and in that farming community. We had a number of people saved, and the Lord gave us a wonderful week of sales at the tape table. On the last night, the pastor came to me and said, "I would have never thought that our people would give like this," and handed me a check for nearly $1,500.

Please keep in mind this was in 1977, and that was a lot of money in those days—particularly for a very small church. I thanked him very kindly and was walking out to the motor home when one of the men, who was a farmer, walked up to me and said, "I want to thank you for coming to our little church and letting God use the team here for His glory." He slipped something into my hand and walked away. When I reached the motor home, we sat down and opened the check that he had given me and found it was for the amount of $2,000. I still believe today that prayer and faith are the answer to our needs and not some church with a guaranteed offering of a certain amount.

The Door That Faith Opened

When we begin to live by faith, we have past experiences of God's miraculous provision from which to draw that will spur us toward believing Him again. Our flesh isn't any different than it was for the children of Israel. They saw God deliver them through the Red Sea and provide many miracles for them, but each time the next test came, their flesh drew back in fear and unbelief. The natural tendency for our flesh *is* to draw back in fear and unbelief, but if we keep close to our memories the miracles God has worked in our lives during past days, it will be a strength to go forward in confidence that He will do it again.

CHAPTER SIX

The Thrills and Trials of Motor Home Life

W HEN MOST PEOPLE SEE SOMEONE traveling full-time in a motor home, particularly a large one, they might imagine it must be one great big vacation. I would think that most people live in some kind of a home which is at least 1,000 square feet or more. Though the big buses were beautiful and very nice, they only had 320 square feet of space. There are a hundred different adjustments for five people living in that small of a space. I think it just comes back to doing for the Lord what you really want to do, and as I said before, it was a great blessing to have our families traveling with us. However, great adjustments needed to be worked out.

The children downsized from having their own rooms and closets to having three bunk beds just off the hall of the motor home, and each had a small enclosed shelf for holding his/her personal items. Three drawers were underneath the bottom bunk and a small closet across the hall for the three of them. The girls shared a small vanity beside the closet which also doubled as a desk for one of them during school. The other two sat at the booth during school, which also served as our dining table.

Pam and I had a bedroom in the back, and we all shared the one bathroom. Our one convenience was a stacked washer and dryer set so we could do laundry without going to a laundromat. In the front of the bus was a couch, the kitchen, the table and one living room chair. Each bus had the same floor plan, and each family of five made the same kind of adjustments to living in a small space.

God soothed our cramped living with quite a lot of humor which helped to make our hearts merry and our homes on wheels cheerful. I'm not sure how many of our readers will be familiar with the country western singer, Tammy Waddell, but one of our humorous incidents involved her. I had a big TW painted on the back of the buses, and each bus had a CB unit to talk to one another while traveling. In those days every trucker had a CB, and one of them came up behind our bus and thought that he was behind Tammy Waddell's bus because of the TW initials painted on the back. Over our CB came these words, "How 'bout that Tammy Waddell up there in that big pretty bus."

I shot back at him, "How about making that Tom Williams, the Gospel preacher," and that was the last we heard from him.

Once in a while Bud and I would get tired, and our wives would drive for us. If you were very careful, it was even possible to switch drivers going down the road, though I do not recommend this. During one particular incident, I was driving our bus, and Mrs. Grinstead was driving their bus a couple hundred yards behind me. Also on the same road about a couple hundred yards apart were two truck drivers. I must preface this incident first by saying that some truck drivers use the term "beaver" when referring to a lady driver. One of these two truck drivers had gotten up alongside of the Grinstead's bus; and as he passed them, he got on the CB and said to the other truck driver, "Check out this good-looking 'beaver' driving the TW bus when you pass by."

When our wives drove, Bud and I always rested somewhere near the front of the bus. After I heard this message on my CB, I told Mrs. Grinstead to change CB channels; while talking on the different channel, I instructed her to wake up Bud and change drivers, which she instantly did. As the second truck driver pulled up alongside the bus, he saw Bud; his response to his buddy was, "What do you mean good-looking beaver? You must be blind; a redneck is driving that bus." As they continued down the road, there was a constant fuss over the CB about which one of them couldn't tell a "beaver" from a "redneck."

We had an unusual circumstance happen one time concerning the trailers Brother Grinstead and I had built for both of us so we could haul our Volkswagen cars behind our motor homes. We were traveling east through Ohio on Interstate 80 one day when out of the corner of my eye, I saw my Volkswagen and trailer traveling right along beside us at 60 miles per hour. I shook my head as I did a double take and blinked my eyes to make sure I was seeing correctly. The trailer tongue took a dive into the dirt, and both trailer and car flipped upside down. I pulled over, and upon getting out and seeing I no longer had a trailer attached to the back of our motor home, I knew my eyes weren't playing tricks on me. Our Volkswagen and trailer were lying smashed in the ditch.

The Lord admonishes us in His Word to give thanks for everything, and just the unusualness of that event caused us to laugh rather than cry. Once we investigated the situation, we discovered that the hitch extending from the motor home to the car had broken in half because of a fault in the metal from its original casting. All things do indeed work together for good, and we thanked the Lord that our insurance company took the hitch to the manufacturer, and they bought us a new car.

A gas station attendant was wonderfully saved late in the evening when we pulled in to refuel. He was admiring our bus when he said to me, "You must be very rich."

My reply was, "No, but my Father is, and He bought this for me."

He made a soft whistle sound and said, "Man, I wish I had a father like that."

I said, "Well, He adopted me, and He is looking for others to adopt." Then I began tell him how God had saved me and how God was the provider of all our needs. It was wonderful to see how ready that gentleman was to receive Christ as Lord and even more wonderful to know that our Heavenly Father led us to him that night.

One comical experience we had, though I must say it didn't seem very funny at the time, was sometime after Pam's illness when we were out in the middle of New Mexico. Phyllis was driving because I was so very tired and sleepy, but we needed to keep going in order to arrive at our next meeting on time. Phyllis had her driver's license and had agreed to drive for me for a while since we were on the open road without much traffic. I showed her the gas pedal and told her how fast to drive; however, I did not show her the brake pedal thinking she would not need it. I told her I would lie down in the aisle of the bus right by her, and she could wake me up very quickly if she needed me. I was soon fast asleep and had only been asleep for a few minutes when I heard Phyllis screaming, "What do I do, Daddy?"

I sat up with a start, and the first thing I saw was three highway patrolmen running to the side of the road to save their lives. They had set up a roadblock and were stopping every vehicle because they were looking for a criminal. Phyllis, not knowing how to use the brakes, drove straight through the temporary roadblock and sent policemen scattering in every direction for cover.

I stopped the bus as quickly as I could, and when the bus came to a stop, the policemen surrounded us with their guns cocked and ready to use. I opened the door very slowly and was allowed to step out. I told them why Phyllis was driving and why she did not stop for the roadblock. It took me a while, but I was finally able to persuade them to believe my story about my sick wife and Phyllis' driving while I rested. The policemen came in and searched the bus. Finally one of them told me I had to follow him into town and stand before the judge at the courthouse. I praise the Lord the judge was very kind and said, "Since you have been brought here, I will have to charge you something." He had me pay a $50 fine and then allowed me to go on my way.

One time while traveling with the Grinsteads to Dallas, Texas, we arrived at the church about 11:00 p.m. and drove the buses to where the pastor had instructed us to park. As Brother Grinstead was backing onto the grass on one side of the church, the rear wheels of the motor home went through the septic tank buried there, and the front end of the motor home was about eight feet off of the ground! The headlights were shining straight up into the air, Mrs. Grinstead and the children were screaming, and the inside of the motor home was immediately rearranged. Though the hour was late, we began to call wrecker services and finally found one that would come to pull the motor home out of the septic tank. Once the motor home was out of the septic tank, we found that there wasn't any damage done to the bus. However, because of the terrible smell, the Grinstead's bus was not a "popular" place to visit. We found out later that the pastor was not knowledgeable about the location of the septic system of the church.

As I have already mentioned, one of the great thrills of life in the motor home was the privilege of having our families with us. There were no goodbyes to say as there had been for so many long years. I don't know about you, but I do not like goodbyes. I know that many times while traveling alone, I didn't think I could face another airplane or the loneliness of staying by myself in the chamber of a church or in a motel. I am sure for some people that might not be a problem, but I was reared in a large family, and we were very close. I missed my wife and children in all those years of traveling by myself, and I remember not being with my oldest son for 12 straight birthdays. To me, those were special occasions, and I advise you that when at all possible, you should be with your loved ones. I missed so many of my children's special school programs, sports events, and things that were tremendously important to family happiness. I also missed being able to be home with my wife and doing things with her and for her as the head of the house.

It was a thrill to be able to homeschool our children as we traveled in the motor home. We started off each day with prayer and pledging allegiance to Old Glory, which to me is a tremendous part of being a Christian and an American. I loved to pray with my family, and anyone who knows me well knows that I am a flag-waving American.

We were able to take wonderful field trips with the children to many manufacturing places, historical sights, and great vacation points in our blessed country. While traveling across the entire nation, including Hawaii, and to the country of Canada, our children were able to visit many sights that most people just read about or see on television. Some of these sights were the many rivers that cross our country, which often mark the boundaries of the states. We were able to see the headwaters of some of the rivers and were able to visit some of the great dams that supply much of our electricity.

We were able to make close friends with thousands of people we would never have met any other way than by being able to park our motor home on their properties during our days off. This would often happen when we would finish a meeting, and someone would invite us to come out to their ranch, their farm, their lakefront property, or their home in a city. These times were so restful for us, and we learned better how to pray for the people to whom we had been ministering.

CHAPTER SIX
The Thrills and Trials of Motor Home Life

I believe I can say without contradiction that the right kinds of friends are one of your greatest assets. I feel so sorry for people who have not invested their life in helping others and learning to know the blessing of being needed and wanted in the lives of others. The motor homes were certainly a great blessing in this way. I would very much recommend to anyone who travels regularly, regardless of how convenient or inconvenient it may be, to take the family also.

Prayer, the Twin Sister of Faith

So MANY TIMES IN SCRIPTURE the Lord tells us that when we pray, we must believe if we are to receive. Mark 11:24 says, *"Therefore I say unto you, What things soever ye desire, when ye pray, believe that ye receive them, and ye shall have them."* This verse is just one example of the many Scriptures that link prayer and faith together.

I remember that my mother prayed so often, and one of her favorite verses was Matthew 6:6. *"But thou, when thou prayest, enter into thy closet, and when thou hast shut thy door, pray to thy Father which is in secret; and thy Father which seeth in secret shall reward thee openly."* This verse tells us that when we pray we need to enter into our closet, and our Father who sees us in secret will reward us openly. I am glad I learned that having a prayer life means spending much time alone with the Lord.

From the time I was saved, the Holy Spirit began to impress upon my heart to learn more about prayer. I began to read about the lives of men like Hudson Taylor, Jonathan Goforth, Adoniram Judson, David Livingston, C.T. Studd, "Praying" John Hyde, Andrew Bonar, William Carey, Andrew Murray, King David, Abraham, Daniel, and of course, our Lord Jesus, and so many others who are named in the Scriptures who devoted countless hours to praying. They understood that which most men never fully grasp.

PRAYER AND FAITH:

The Life of Dr. Tom Williams

I developed my prayer life as a cross-country runner in training would gradually lengthen his distance. I did not try to go from 10 or 15 minutes of prayer to an hour. I did not try to go from an hour to several hours. In His wonderful grace, God lengthened, widened, and deepened my burden to pray.

One of the greatest lessons, or perhaps it is the greatest lesson, that I ever learned was to get up when the Lord woke me up. I wish I could say that I mastered that quickly or even now have mastered it, but I am like Paul who pressed toward the mark. I began to ask the Lord to wake me up during the night if He needed someone to pray.

The story of a missionary friend of mine named Fred in India certainly ingrained this lesson into my life. Shortly after Fred arrived in India, he was in the bush country where he was attacked by a mad elephant. Fred began to run, but the elephant was gaining in his pursuit. A man suddenly appeared on a hill in front of the fleeing missionary. The man was making motions with his hands which directed Fred to run in a zigzag fashion. As soon as Fred veered from his straight path, he very quickly was able to escape the elephant. (I have been told that elephants follow by smell, and the elephant could not turn as quickly as Fred could.)

He told me that after reaching a point of safety, he looked at the hill once again and found no one there. He quickly made his way to the top of the hill and looked in every direction as far as he could see and still found no one. He shared with me that several weeks later he received a letter from his mother in America, and she had written, "Freddy, during a certain night the Lord woke me up and impressed upon me that you were in great danger and that I should pray."

Fred said that he had calculated the time difference, and it was at that exact time that the unknown man appeared on the top of the hill.

When he told me the story, I said, "Fred that had to be an

angel." The thought that gripped my heart then and still grips my heart today is, "What if his mother had not prayed?"

I would challenge you to let the simple truth of getting up when the Lord wakes you up be a great factor in learning to pray. There are no short cuts in a life of prayer; and in spite of many modern teachings that say it isn't how long you pray, it's how you pray, you will never reach the prayer life of our Saviour until you learn to spend hours in prayer.

In Matthew 14, after the Lord Jesus told His disciples to get in the boat and go to the other side, He went alone up into a mountain. The Scripture says He went there to pray. The Bible continues on to say that Jesus came walking on the water in the fourth watch, which is sometime between 3:00 and 6:00 in the morning. I would guess that when He fed the 5,000, it would have been sometime in the afternoon. If He went to the mountain to pray at 4:00 p.m. and did not come walking on the water until the fourth watch, He had been in prayer approximately 12 hours.

The Bible says in Luke 6:12 that on another occasion the Lord Jesus went into the mountain to pray and continued all night in prayer. The Scriptures tell us in Mark 1:35 that Jesus rose a great while before day and went out to pray in a solitary place. These instances lead me to believe that the Saviour put great emphasis on the longevity of prayer.

Daniel 10 gives an account of Daniel's being in prayer for 21 days. In Nehemiah 1, the Bible states that Nehemiah prayed and fasted certain days. David prayed seven days before his baby died. If I summarize all these Biblical instances of prayer with great historical examples like Praying Hyde's going into a closet for six days and only coming out for necessary times, and add so many other men's lives who prayed days at a time, I am absolutely persuaded you will never learn to call down the power of God without the longevity of prayer. I am sure at this point someone will say Elijah prayed on Mt. Carmel, and the rain came. We could turn yet to other places in the Scripture where men and women prayed, and God answered immediately. These prayers and the answer to them were backed by lives of prayer as we see in I Samuel 1 when God answered Hannah's prayer. God did answer Hannah's prayer with Eli's saying God would give her a son, but a careful reading of this passage reveals she had been praying for years for this child.

Some years ago a lady called who heard I had a life of prayer. She told me she had read many different books on the subject of prayer by both contemporary authors and authors of years ago. She asked me what I might teach her about prayer. My question to her was, "How much do you pray?"

She replied, "Perhaps an hour a day." I told her she could read all the books that had ever been written, but praying is the only way to learn to pray. This is where most people draw the line on really wanting to have a prayer life.

I remember a young man's picking me up at an airport as I was flying into Washington, D.C., to speak at a banquet. He asked me, "What would be the one thing you would advise me as a college student and a young man seeking to serve God?"

I'm sure he thought I would tell him to build a great library or perhaps to study more and more, and certainly either one of these or even both are commendable ideas. I said, "Young man, if I told you what would be the greatest help to you now and all of your life, you would not do it." He very readily assured me that his question was sincere, and he would do whatever I told him. My answer to him was, "You need to begin to build a prayer life of several hours a day."

"I can't do that," he said. "I'm going to school 40 hours a week and working 40 hours a week. I cannot do what you are suggesting."

"I told you that you wouldn't do what I was going to tell you."

CHAPTER SEVEN

Prayer, The Twin Sister of Faith

This is the dead-end street that I run into in most people's lives who think they want to have a life of prayer. What I find is that most people want me to do their praying for them. I am thrilled that over the years God has miraculously answered thousands of prayers when I have prayed. I am thankful that people want me to bear their burdens before the Lord. It is a great joy to be an intercessor on behalf of others. But however great the answers are, it does not teach them to pray. It simply attests to the fact that God does hear *"The effectual, fervent prayer of a righteous man."* (James 5:16) Oh, how wonderful it would be if there was a thirst for the prayer closet in America and around the world in the hearts of God's people!

I wish we could understand that the Bible does not major on preaching; rather, it majors on praying. I wish we could come to grips with the fact that the Bible says in Isaiah 56:7, *"...mine house shall be called an house of prayer."* This truth is reiterated in Matthew 21:13 and a number of other places in the Scriptures. Not by our wildest imagination could we believe that we would be honest in writing over the doors of our churches, "This is a house of prayer." How empty a statement, "This is a football field," would be if football had never or would never be played on that field. Great football teams go to that stadium to practice and practice and practice, which is how they become champions. I would to God that God's people would wear out the carpet at the altars and leave their tear stains because they have sought the God of Heaven day after day.

The story is told of a young man who was coming in from between our lines and the enemy's lines during World War II. One of his fellow soldiers saw him coming in from this position and at gunpoint took him to the captain of that regiment. He told the captain that this man was a traitor and had been out conferring with the enemy. The captain asked the young soldier if this was true, and the soldier answered, "No, Sir." The captain then asked the soldier why

s1

he was out there, and the soldier answered, "Sir, it was the only quiet place I could find to pray to God." The captain then told the soldier to get down on his knees and start praying. The young soldier knelt down and began to pray and weep as he cried out to his Heavenly Father. The captain touched the young man on the shoulder after 45 minutes and said, "You are free to go. Had you not been so often in practice, you would not have done so well in drill." When people hear you pray, can they really believe that you actually are talking with God?

I remember being in a church in Washington state, and I was meeting with the men of the church each morning at 6:00 to pray. On the third day, one of the men from the church asked the pastor, "Would it be okay with you if just Brother Williams prayed? It is so evident that God hears him." I do not tell this story or any other story to gratify my flesh, but as Paul said in Philippians 3 concerning his life for Christ, that it might cause the brethren to understand his life in Christ. So the pastor consented, and each morning I prayed for an hour to an hour and a half as the men listened and prayed, I'm sure, in their hearts along with me.

While I was living in California, one young man named Bob said to me, "I understand that sometimes you pray all night." I told him that I did on occasion pray all night. He asked if I ever let anyone come and pray with me. I said, "Not usually, but if you would like to come, we will pray all night together." What happened was very humorous to me. We began praying about 9:00 p.m., and at midnight, we stopped to have a cup of hot chocolate, and then returned to prayer until 3:00 a.m. We were alternating in prayer, and it was his turn to pray when he said, "God, I don't have another thing to talk to You about."

I said, "Bob, then it is time to go home." He and I have laughed about that through the years.

Prayer, The Twin Sister of Faith

A wonderful experience occurred while I was the youth pastor in Hemet, California. Two men from the church came to me and asked, "Is it true that you pray early every morning? If it is, would we be able to come and pray with you?" I told them that I had never tried having someone pray with me, and I was not sure how it would work but that we would try it for a few weeks. The men began coming to pray with me early every morning, and we prayed together for about six weeks. One of them read meters for the city of Hemet, and the other man drove an 18-wheel truck hauling hay. During that short period of time, the Lord called both of those men to preach; they surrendered to go to Bible college. Both of them have been in the ministry now for many years.

Some people would say prayer is not that which motivates you to serve God; rather, it is a crutch in the Christian life. They would believe that prayer does not form a person's Christian life, but it is just a help in getting through the Christian life. William Carey, that great man of prayer and the man who is called the father of mission work as we now know it, prayed countless hours for every nation as well as for the great servants of God of that day. Prayer drove William Carey to India and to conquer it for Christ. I met a family from India while I was preaching in a church at Valley Forge, Pennsylvania, and they told me they were descendants of a family saved during the time William Carey labored for Christ in India. Nothing is more lasting than the effects of people who are saved in answer to prayer.

CHAPTER EIGHT

⚮

Answers From Heaven

THE SCRIPTURE SAYS IN JEREMIAH 33:3, "*Call unto me, and I will answer thee, and shew thee great and mighty things, which thou knowest not.*" In Luke 18:1 our Lord Jesus said that, "*…men ought always to pray, and not to faint.*" In this same chapter the Lord Jesus tells the parable about the widow woman and her perseverance in obtaining an answer. As you seek answers from the Lord, I encourage you to be faithful in your asking and to persevere. The Lord wants us to pray about everything—which is exactly what I have sought to do over the years.

One day I was seated next to a lady on a flight to Arizona; and as soon as the plane took off, I began to make conversation with her about the Lord. She told me she was the owner of a large restaurant in Tucson, Arizona. She was a world traveler, and she was returning from an overseas tour. She told me about the church she attended and about her religious beliefs, but she didn't know about salvation in Christ. She agreed to let me show her what God says in His Word concerning salvation and eternal life. As I unfolded the Scriptures to her by the power of the Holy Spirit, it was evident that God was beginning to open her eyes and that He was moving upon her heart.

She asked, "Do you mean that I can be saved here on this airplane and know for sure that I am God's child, that my sins are forgiven, and that I will have a home in Heaven?"

I answered, "Yes, Ma'am, you surely can." She wonderfully

received Jesus Christ as her personal Saviour, and immediately the burden of her sin was lifted from her.

I was going to Phoenix to speak in a church there, and the assistant pastor met me at the airport. As he was coming to greet me, this lady stepped in front of me and said to him, "Are you here to pick up Dr. Williams?"

He answered, "I am."

She said to the assistant pastor, "Are you saved?"

He assured her that he knew Jesus Christ as his Lord and Saviour.

She said, "This man has taught me more about God on this flight than my church has taught me in 45 years." She shared with him how she had been saved and then handed me a business card saying, "If you and your family are ever through Tucson, please stop at the restaurant."

About one year later my family and I were passing through Tucson on our way to Texas, so we stopped to have supper at her restaurant. It was a beautiful Italian restaurant, and I think every waiter was told to bring us something. We didn't even get a chance to order our food; she just started sending it out. After we had eaten all we possibly could, she then began to send out several kinds of desserts. We had a long conversation with her, and then I asked for the bill as we had to be on our way.

She said, "Mr. Williams, you cannot pay for anything in a restaurant that you own."

I said, "I don't own this restaurant."

She said, "Yes, you do, because you told me about how to be saved through the Lord Jesus Christ. Please stop as often as you can, and there will never be a charge."

⊗⊗

In my travels over the years, I have always asked the Lord to allow me to witness to someone for Him. One of those answers to prayer came in the Greensboro, North Carolina, airport. I saw a young man dressed in a semi-Western style. I walked over to him and asked if he had horses.

"Yes," he said, "I have a number of very nice quarter horses." He asked me if I knew anything about quarter horse bloodlines, and I told him of several quarter horses that I had owned that came from excellent bloodlines.

He said, "You do know something about quarter horses."

"Yes, I have ridden many and have shown quite a few, but there is something I do now that is far greater."

"What would that be?"

"I tell folks everywhere I go about the Lord Jesus Christ," I replied.

He told me that he was a Christian and that he and his dad were traveling together on the same plane my wife and I would be on. He told his dad of our conversation; upon boarding the plane, we found out their seats were immediately behind ours. Once we were in the air, this man's dad asked me if I really was a preacher. I assured him of the many years that I had been an evangelist. He commented to me that it was a rare combination to find someone like me who was not only a preacher, but also knowledgeable about quarter horses. The seat beside me was empty, so he asked if he might come up and sit beside me for a while. As we began to talk he said, "How do you make a living as an evangelist?"

I replied that I travel to churches, preach, and they give me a love offering. I also told him that the Lord had asked me to live by faith. He then asked me if he could help faith out.

I said, "If the Lord has put that on your heart, that would be wonderful." He then proceeded to give me a check for $1,500. After giving me the money, he told me that he owned a chain of Western clothing stores and that he wanted me and my family to visit any of his stores whenever we needed clothing. He gave me his personal card telling me this would be as good as having cash to purchase the items we needed. For several years most of the clothing that we wore came from the generosity of this good man.

On another occasion, my wife and I had gone to Hawaii to get some much needed rest and to preach in one of the island churches. I was sitting one day reading my Bible by the ocean when a gentleman came walking by and said, "You're reading the Good Book."

I replied, "No," and continued reading.

He had already walked by me a couple of steps, but upon realizing what I had said, he came back. He asked me, "Is that the Bible?"

"Yes, it is," I replied.

He inquired, "Isn't that a good book?"

I said, "No, Sir."

He then asked me, "What kind of book is it?"

I smiled and answered, "It's the best book!" He then asked if he could sit and talk with me, and I told him that he could. During our conversation, he asked, "Do you and your wife have any plans for this evening?" When I told him we did not, he said, "My wife and I would like to take you and your wife out for dinner tonight."

Without any hesitation, I said, "We would like to accept your invitation." While we were at dinner, they told us of their conversion to the Lord Jesus Christ, and we had a wonderful meal and fellowship with them. At their request we went with them to their condo following the meal to continue our enjoyable fellowship and conversation which centered on the Lord.

As my wife and I were getting ready to say goodnight and leave, he asked me to lead in prayer, so I knelt down on my knees as I usually do and prayed for approximately 15 minutes.

When I finished praying, he said, "I like that."

I said, "I'm glad."

He then asked about our lunch plans for the next day. When I told him we did not have plans, he said, "We would like to take you to lunch."

"We would like to go."

During lunch the next day, he asked me if we came to Hawaii every year. I answered, "Yes," and then explained that I preached in the small churches on the island that cannot afford to have a special speaker come. "Next year my entire family will be coming with me, and I will be preaching on four of the islands."

He said, "That sure will take a lot of money. After lunch you better go for a ride with me in my car." I agreed to do so, and we drove with him to what is called Napili Shores Condominiums. As we walked into the offices of the condominiums, everyone began to greet him by name. By that time I thought that it sure didn't hurt to be with this gentleman. We walked up to the desk clerk, and he asked the clerk to put my family and me in two of the condos the next year for five weeks! I calculated in my head what a stay like that would cost, and I came up with a figure that equaled several thousands of dollars. Realizing what started all this, I am convinced it pays to read your Bible.

The Lord presented another unique situation for us when we returned to Hawaii the following year. I had been preaching on the island of Kauai and had just returned to Maui where my family and I were staying when my wife said to me, "Sweetheart, I met this couple, and I think you might win them to Christ."

I went over and began to talk to the man and noticed that he was reading the book of Mormon. I asked him, "Are you Mormon, or are you just reading the book?"

He answered, "I'm not a Mormon; I'm just looking for the truth."

I told him that he had the wrong book. He asked me if I had the right book, and I assured him that I did. Then I asked him and his wife to come to our condo with me. For three and one-half hours, they asked me questions regarding their religious backgrounds, and as fast as I could turn the pages in the Bible, I gave them a scriptural answer to their questions.

Finally, the man looked at his wife and said, "Do you have any more questions?"

She said, "No."

He then said, "We should get saved through the Lord Jesus Christ." He was a building contractor from Regina, Saskatchewan, Canada. As soon as my family and I returned to the mainland and to our home in Colorado, I mailed two beautiful study Bibles to this couple. Shortly after that, I received a $2,000 check for our ministry from them. I often tell people that was the best Bible sales I've ever made.

For the next two years, this dear couple sent frequent checks to help us to get out the Gospel of the Lord Jesus Christ. Then one day I received a letter from them that said, "Brother Williams, there won't be any more checks; we are going to Bible college."

I lost touch with them for a few years, and then in 1993 I received one of the most thrilling letters of my entire ministry. He wrote, "Brother Williams, I don't think that when you led me to Christ you knew that I spoke perfect Russian. When the curtain fell in Russia, God called my wife and me to go there and reach the people for Christ. I began to rent auditoriums across Russia and preach salvation through Christ Jesus. At the writing of this letter, we have had 375,000 Russians bow their head to receive the Lord Jesus Christ as their Saviour." This couple came to our home in 1995 and spent Christmas with us. What a blessing it was as they said, "We just wanted to see our spiritual daddy again." God really does do abundantly above all that we can ask or think.

≈

I was walking across a Bible college campus one day when I saw a young man coming toward me, and the Lord directed my eyes to his shoes. I had prayed that morning as I usually do that the Lord would make me a blessing in someone's life. The young man's shoes were completely worn out, and I don't know that I've ever seen anyone continue to wear shoes that were in that bad of shape. The Lord spoke to my heart and said, "He needs some new shoes."

I replied, "He really does, Father." The Lord told me to buy him a pair of new shoes, so I proceeded to ask this young man if he had any time open that morning, and he said he was available at 11:00 a.m. I went to the school office and obtained permission to take him off campus, and then I took him to a Florshiem shoe store and bought him a beautiful pair of shoes.

On the drive back to the college he said, "The shoes that I had been wearing had been my father's shoes before he passed away, but my mother had him buried barefooted so I could have some shoes to wear at school. I have worn them until, as you saw, they were completely falling apart because I couldn't afford to buy new shoes." With tears in his eyes he asked me, "How did you know it was my birthday?"

I replied, "Son, I did not know it was your birthday. I bought the shoes because the Lord told me to."

He said, "Since it is my birthday and my dad is no longer living, do you think it would be okay if I called you 'Dad' the rest of this day?" As tears were pouring down my cheeks, I thanked my Heavenly Father and told the young man, "You sure can."

≈

PRAYER AND FAITH:
The Life of Dr. Tom Williams

I went to Alaska one year to preach and to hunt with two businessmen, Brother Donny and Brother Dick. We flew into Anchorage on a Saturday, and I preached at Anchorage Baptist Temple on Sunday. On Monday we charted a float plane to take us 175 miles into the recesses of Northwest Alaska; however, 40 miles out we flew into a thick fog bank and had to return to Anchorage. Tuesday we were able to fly out and get beyond the mountain pass; however, we still were unable to reach our initial destination because of the fog. The pilot turned and took us to a lake south of the one intended; and after unloading all our gear, he faithfully promised he would pick us up on Thursday. I said, "I have to preach on statewide television Sunday, so I must be back to Anchorage for that."

He replied, "Oh, I'll have you out in plenty of time."

We set up camp and began to scout out the territory for caribou and black bear that afternoon. Wednesday morning we were able to get two caribou and one black bear that afternoon. Thursday afternoon we were packed and waiting for the plane down by the shore; however, the plane didn't arrive. Neither did the plane arrive that evening, so we set up our tents once more and thought for sure he would be there the next day.

Friday we woke up hopeful; however, the day went by without the arrival of the plane. When the plane wasn't there Saturday morning, we began to get concerned. Donnie had hurt his back packing the bear out of the canyon and was extremely uncomfortable. Our food was nearly gone, and the weather was growing colder.

By the time Sunday morning arrived and the plane still wasn't there, frightening thoughts began to plague us. "Perhaps the pilot crashed and never made it back to Anchorage," or "No one knows where we are because we are not on the lake the pilot had marked on the map;" these thoughts began to run constantly through our minds. Snow had also begun to fall earlier that morning, and the stories I'd heard of only two men surviving the walk out of the recesses of the back country of Alaska gripped my heart with fear. To keep warm we remained in our sleeping bags inside our tent. By early afternoon Donny enthusiastically said, "I hear the plane coming!" All three of us jumped up and excitedly ran out to watch the plane land; however, there wasn't any plane. Donny had only imagined the drone of an engine because we all wanted so badly to hear one.

About an hour later, Dick said, "I hear it, and it's for real this time." Again we all ran out of the tent, but there still wasn't any plane landing on the lake. With disappointment we returned to the tent, and I said to the men, "You guys go to the tent; I'm going out here to these elder bushes and get a hold of the Lord about our situation."

I fell on my knees and had been praying about 30 minutes when I heard the plane's engine and jumped up shouting, "Thank You, Heavenly Father!" as I ran as fast as I could down to the lake. My heart was pounding in my chest with excitement and jubilation that we were finally being rescued.

As the plane landed and taxied near to the shore, I reached out my hand and took hold of the wing strut to pull it in closer. When my hand touched that strut, the Spirit of God spoke to me so vividly, it was as though a spear had pierced my soul. He said, "Tom, have you ever wanted the Lord Jesus to come as badly as you wanted that plane to come?"

I knew in my heart it would be a lie to say that I had. I ran back up the hill and fell on my knees in our little cook tent, telling my Heavenly Father how ashamed I was and that in the future I would constantly look for the coming of the Lord Jesus. While we were flying back to Anchorage, I asked the pilot, "Why didn't you come back for us on Thursday like you promised? You knew I was scheduled to preach in Anchorage this morning."

He answered saying, "I'm really sorry about this. I had started back on Thursday to get you; however, as I took off on the lake in Anchorage, my engine blew up about 300 feet in the air. I had to drop back onto the lake. I tried to borrow a similar plane, but all the outfitters were using them. Finally, today I was able to get this plane to come get you."

I do not know why this all happened, but I do know that God is in charge of our lives. Brother Dick also learned a very valuable lesson as one night at the camp, we were sitting by the campfire and he said to Donny and me, "I could buy a number of those planes, but I don't see them for sale. This is the first time in my life when my money is not the answer to my predicament." As I close this story, let me ask you, "How long has it been since you really wanted the Lord Jesus to come?"

⟡

Over the years many ladies have asked me to pray for them to be able to have children. I received a letter signed by six ladies from North Carolina, asking me to pray for them to have babies. The letter said, "We have heard from others how God granted them children in answer to your prayers, and we would like you to pray for us." I wrote them and told them I would faithfully pray for one year that God would grant them the desire of their hearts and give them each a child. One year later these ladies wrote to thank me for praying. In the letter they wrote that five of the ladies had given birth, and one lady gave birth to twins. I thank the Lord for His mighty power.

⟡

I was preaching in Maryland one time when a man and his wife spoke to me following an evening service. They said, "We desire children, but the doctors have told us that we are not able to have them. We know you are a man of prayer, and we would like you to pray for us." The three of us went to an empty room in the church and bowing on our knees, went before the Lord with their request. Following prayer, I asked them if they would go home and build a nursery, by faith, for the baby. Ten months later I received a letter from this same couple telling me she had given birth to twins. There was a post script in the letter from her husband which said, "Please quit praying!" Such answers to prayer cause one to burst into song singing, "O Lord my God…how great Thou art."

Not long after I started in evangelism, I was preaching in a Christian youth camp; at the end of the week, the man in charge told me, "Brother Williams, we never pay any of our speakers until the end of the summer. At that time we split the offering equally among all those who have preached for us here at the camp." I was already financially strapped, and I had to travel from Indiana to Chattanooga, Tennessee, where I was to attend a conference. I had been planning on the love offering to help me get to Tennessee and to take care of other necessities. I only had a total of $20 with me when on the morning of the last day of camp, the Lord said to me, "Tom, I want you to give the cook half of your $20." The cook for the camp was a lady, and she had asked some of us to pray for her as she had some very pressing financial needs. The Lord also said to me, "If you will give this to her, I will give you $200." I gave the lady the $10 for which she was so very thankful, and the Lord provided for me as He promised.

A pastor, who had been at the camp with some of his young people, spoke to me and said, "Brother Williams, I heard you mention that you need to go to Chattanooga for a conference. The Lord has laid it on my heart to drive you to the conference and to stay to attend it as well. It will not cost you anything."

When we left the camp, we had only gone ten miles when the pastor said, "I have to stop at this little Mom and Pop grocery store."

When he came out of the store and got back into the car, he pitched an envelope in my lap and told me it was for me.

I said, "I already know what it is in this envelope. There is $200 inside this envelope."

He asked, "How did you know that?"

I then told him the story of how God had asked me to give the $10 and that He would give me $200." A businessman had been at camp, and God had touched his heart to give me some money. This businessman had told the pastor and had asked him to pick up the money at this store when we left camp. Heaven had once again come to my rescue!

              ⟳⟲

When my first wife passed away in California, my pastor at that time was so very thoughtful and kind. He preached my wife's funeral and then also my daughter's funeral a few months later. He, his wife, and their family were such a help and encouragement to me and became very special friends to my family and me.

As the years passed, our friendship remained, and our roles reversed as I was able to help preach his funeral when he went home to be with the Lord.

Following his death, I often would see his dear wife when I was preaching in California, and she would always say to me, "Tommy, I want you to remember that I want you to preach my funeral when that time comes."

In the late 1990s I received a call from one of her daughters asking me if I would come and preach the funeral as her mother had just passed away. This was another time when our finances were extremely tight, and I didn't have any money to buy an airplane ticket to go to the funeral. I knew I had to beseech Heaven once again, so I went to my closet to pray. While in my closet, the Devil said to me, "If you get on that plane to go preach that funeral, I will kill you."

My Heavenly Father reminded me that He was in charge of life and death—not Satan. I borrowed $800 and flew to California for the funeral.

The funeral was so blessed of God, and her children were over-whelmed with what the Lord did with the message. One of them handed me an envelope and said, "This is from us. Thank you for coming."

In the envelope was $1,000, which gave me enough to pay off the ticket and have an extra $200. I had three hours before I had to return to the airport and catch my plane home, so at the request of the children, I attended the reception following the funeral service.

I saw some people at the reception I had not seen in years. One lady in particular asked if I remembered her, and I said I did and called her by name.

During our conversation she said, "Tommy, do you need some money?"

I said, "I don't know why you're asking, but yes, I sure do."

She then asked me, "How much do you need?"

I replied, "I wouldn't want to blow your mind."

"Try blowing it," she said. Since she had asked, I told her, "If I had $50,000 right now, I could only go home and bring our ministry's needs up-to-date."

She said, "Tommy, I don't have $50,000, but I have been doing very well as a realtor. If you will pray that God would give me a sale with a $50,000 commission, I will give it to you."

I said to her, "Let's pray right now," and I prayed, "Heavenly Father, would You please bless this dear lady with a sale that would bring in $50,000 as she would like to give it to the ministry. Would You then bless her ten times over and bring in a sale that would give her $500,000 for her own needs?" I continued to pray in the weeks follow-ing, and during the third week I was walking from the office to the house when the mailman drove into our driveway, asked me to sign for a piece of mail, and then handed me a registered letter. I opened the envelope, and with tears falling from my cheeks, I saw that it was a certified check in the amount of $50,000! The power of God in answering prayer and in providing such a tremendous need so overwhelmed me that I fell immediately to my knees there on the pavement and raised my hands toward Heaven, praising Almighty God.

Two years later this same lady flew from California to Tennessee where I was preaching at the time. She said, "Tommy, I came here today because God did what you asked Him to do and gave me the $500,000, and I want to give your ministry another gift." She then handed me a check for the amount of $52,000. "The extra $2,000 is for the blessed, sweet lady that takes care of Pam," she explained. Our Heavenly Father so often does exceedingly, abundantly above what we ask or think.

We were in a small church in the Atlanta, Georgia, area during the Christmas season when God once more demonstrated that His arm does not wax short nor is His power diminished. The preacher's wife came to me and said, "Brother Williams, my dad sent us $240 so our children could have gifts at Christmas. I believe, however, that God wants us to give you this money for your willingness to come here, but my husband does not agree and does not want to give you this money. Would you tell him that I know it is from the Lord and we ought to give it?"

I replied, "No, it isn't my place or your place to tell your husband. The Lord will have to speak to him."

That evening the pastor said to me, "I know my wife is right and that God wants you to have this money."

I was moved to tears and silently cried out from my heart to my Heavenly Father asking Him, "What do I do?"

The Lord led me to take both of them by the hand, and I prayed this prayer, "Thank You, Lord, for the $240 this dear couple is sacrificially giving to our ministry. May you please give them, by Christmas, 100 times this amount they have given?"

I was sitting in my office on Christmas Eve when the phone rang. When I answered it, I heard the sound of a sobbing lady. It was the pastor's wife from the little church in Atlanta. She said, "Brother Williams, I have just opened a letter containing $24,000 for our Christmas. It is exactly 100 times what God led us to give you!" Even as I write this book, my heart cries out, "Hallelujah! Hallelujah! What a mighty God we serve!"

During our move in 1999 from Murfreesboro, Tennessee, to Belgrade, Montana, God again tried our faith right up to the midnight hour. Our offer on a beautiful house had been accepted. The owner had verbally agreed to allow us to move into the house with nothing down, and I would pay him one week later when my money had cleared escrow in Tennessee. We had three large rental trucks, a car hauler, two pickups, and a van loaded to capacity the day we were driving out of Murfreesboro when we received a phone call telling me the offer now was being declined.

His realtor had told him, "Christian or no Christian, you should not let this man move into your house without having received your money." Of course, this wasn't the news we wanted to receive as we pulled out of Tennessee, but I knew there was no turning back; God was still leading us to Montana.

As we made our way across the country, our daughter Penny was working feverishly with a banker she knew in Bozeman to secure a loan for us. Penny's excellent credit with that bank was the key in our getting the loan because he took her word that I also would be a safe risk. Therefore, he decided to loan me the money. I needed to sign the loan papers in time for Penny to get the affirmation from the bank and deliver the papers to the owner of the house. However, we were driving through Wyoming at that time—an obstacle because the towns in Wyoming were few and far apart. It is wonderful that there aren't any obstacles to God, and He is always able to provide a way when it would appear hopeless to us.

We were only about an hour out of Sheridan when Penny called and told me she was faxing the loan papers to a particular hotel there, and I could stop, sign them, and then fax them back to her. Once she received the papers and the bank approved them, she was then able to get them to the owner in plenty of time. By the time we drove into Belgrade, the home was now ours. God's peace filled my soul, and I lifted my hands toward Heaven, thanking Him that I had a place to unload all our possessions, but most of all that I had a home in which to take care of my invalid wife.

God may lead us into uncertain circumstances that appear hopeless like He did when He led Moses and the children of Israel to the Red Sea. But as He leads, He is teaching us to fall further upon Him in prayer, believing He will intervene miraculously for us. Dire circumstances produce a further dependency upon our prayer-answering Father. He will not lead where He does not go.

While we were living in Belgrade, Montana, the ministry was experiencing another season of financial difficulty. We had spent hours of fervent prayer beseeching God to intervene; however, God chose to test and strengthen our faith further by delaying the answer. One day in April, I went to the mailbox and found a large manila envelope from a very good friend. Inside I found a Christmas card and a note explaining why I was receiving a Christmas card in April. My friend wrote, "I sent you this card in December; I don't know where it's been, but it was just returned to me a week ago. It was quite puzzling to me, but God made it clear when He said, 'This card didn't reach Tom because you didn't put any money in it.' So please find enclosed a check for $10,000. I trust this amount is sufficient enough that the Lord will deliver it this time."

Needless to say, it was a tremendous encouragement to our souls. His ways are not our ways, but they are always the right ways.

I was asked by some men in North Carolina during 1990 to take them to the West on motorcycles because they had heard of my love for motorcycle riding and knew I was familiar with the western states. I agreed to take them, so one of the men who owned a motorcycle shop loaned me a beautiful Harley-Davidson motorcycle to ride. A total of seven of us put on helmets and tested the headsets, making sure we could communicate with one another the morning we rode out of Winston-Salem, North Carolina.

I was led of the Holy Spirit to ask our Heavenly Father to protect us and to keep it from raining on us the entire trip. A couple of men in the group were not saved, and I wanted them to see there is a God Who will hear and answer prayer. When I finished praying, I heard a quiet snicker come from those men. I knew they were thinking, "Ride 6,000 miles and not get rained on? That preacher must be crazy."

We had a wonderful trip and saw such sights as the St. Louis Arch, Pike's Peak in Colorado, Mt. Rushmore in South Dakota, Glacier National Park in Montana, and Yellowstone National Park in Wyoming. All praise to the name of the Lord, for 6,000 miles we never had one drop of rain fall on us! We saw where it had rained in front of us; we saw it raining on both sides of us, but it never rained on us! I am reminded of the Scripture in the book of James, "*...yet ye have not, because ye ask not.*" (James 4:2) I believe God wants to show His power if we would only ask Him in faith believing. Once we were back in North Carolina, all the men told me, "We never really expected that to happen." Those men told that story to a multitude of motorcycle riders they knew.

～～

It was Pam's birthday, and we were traveling in our motor home on our way to one of the southern states. We didn't have any money to celebrate her birthday, but I gathered the children together and said, "Children, we need to pray and ask God to provide because it is Mother's birthday and we need to do something special for her." As we continued on our way south, the Lord spoke to my heart to take a particular exit off of the freeway. At the bottom of this exit, we saw a hotel and restaurant, and the Lord said to me, "Tom, take your family into that restaurant and celebrate Pam's birthday."

I reminded Him that we didn't have any money; He reminded me that He was very much aware of our financial situation, and He would take care of the bill. We went to that restaurant, and the children and I told Pam to order something very special because we were celebrating her birthday. Just as we were finishing our meal, the manager of the restaurant walked over to our table and said, "Ever since you came in the restaurant, I have been trying to figure out who you are. It has been several years since I heard you speak, but I believe you are Brother Tom Williams."

I said, "Yes, Sir, that is who I am."

He said, "I could not tell you what a privilege it would be for me to pay for your meals."

I proceeded to tell him how the Lord had directed me to this restaurant and that we had come in, sat down, ordered, and ate our meals absolutely by faith. He was overjoyed to think that he was the answer to a prayer! I knew just how he felt as I often have wondered if the greatest joy is having a prayer answered or if it is being the answer to a prayer. I wonder how long it has been since you have been an answer to a prayer.

∽⌒∾

In flying approximately five million miles in a period of forty years, there were so many answers to prayer. The Lord kept me through situation after situation. One such situation occurred during a flight to Atlanta, Georgia. The plane was prepared to land and was committed to landing when the plane violently vibrated and shook as the pilot had suddenly given the plane full throttle power. Gradually, it rose back up into the air, and the vibrating stopped.

The pilot's voice was heard over the intercom saying, "I'm sorry, ladies and gentlemen, but a small private plane turned in front of us to land where we had been given clearance, and we would have collided had I not pulled out immediately as I did." We resumed our position for landing once more, were given clearance to land, and had committed to land when the same violent vibrating occurred again. This time the pilot came over the loud speaker and said, "I'm really sorry, but we were landing right behind an Air Force fighter jet, and the jet's parachute came loose and headed straight toward us." Praise the Lord, on the third attempt at landing we landed safely!

∽⌒∾

On one of my flights home to Denver, Colorado, the plane's kitchen burst into flames, filling the cabin with smoke about 25 miles out from the airport. We were given directions as to what we were to do to prepare for a quick landing and immediate evacuation once on the ground; we were told not to take anything with us but only to be concerned with exiting the plane safely and as quickly as possible. Once we had landed, all the passengers were able to disembark without difficulty, and the ground crew was able to safely extinguish the fire. Praise God there wasn't any harm to anyone on the plane!

PRAYER AND FAITH:
The Life of Dr. Tom Williams

We were coming in to the Kansas City, Missouri, airport one time when I noticed that the pilot had flown over the airport at about 1,000 feet in the air. For those who have not flown very much, it's a recognized fact that pilots do not take this action unless something is wrong. The pilot flew out about another ten miles and announced, "Ladies and gentlemen, I flew over the airport because we have a landing gear that will not release. I wanted the men in the tower to check and see if they saw anything wrong. The airport ground crew is preparing the runway and assembling emergency vehicles because I am going to have to make an emergency landing."

I had been reading my Bible for most of the flight and still had it open when a man sitting near me said, "Preacher, read a little of that to me." A lady sitting behind me and a gentleman two seats behind me asked me to read the Bible to them as well. Not long after these requests a gentleman, who was halfway back in the plane, stood up, and said, "Rev., just let that drift all over the plane."

As I began to read the Bible to all of the passengers, a stewardess tapped me on the shoulder and said, "The pilot just instructed me to open the cabin door so he and the copilot could hear the reading of the Bible also."

After I read some of the Bible to the entire plane, I then asked them to bow their heads. I prayed and asked the Lord to make the faulty landing gear descend and lock into place. I told everyone on the plane that I believed the Lord had heard my prayer and that this would indeed happen.

As we neared the runway, the pilot purposely allowed the plane to drop the last few feet down onto the one locked landing gear in hopes it would dislodge the wheel that would not release and lock into place. The sudden impact upon the working landing gear did indeed jar the faulty one, causing it to finally lower and lock into place. We taxied safely down the runway.

I said to the people on the plane, "Do not say, 'We sure were lucky,' but thank God for the safety of your lives today." I praise God that the Bible says, "*God is...a very present help in trouble.*"(Psalm 46:1)

On a flight I was on to Buffalo, New York, the Lord would not let me be silent when I heard a businessman and a young college student who were sitting behind me discussing the problems America was facing. The businessman had asked the college student why there was such a deluge of dope, promiscuity, and crime in America. The college student philosophized for several minutes and basically said nothing. At this point I stood up with my Bible in my hand and said to the businessman, "I would like to answer the question that you asked this young man a few minutes ago."

He said, "I would like an answer."

As I held up my Bible, I said, "The reason America is in such trouble is that America has forgotten this Book and the God Who wrote this book."

The college student looked at me and stated, "You do not know for a fact that God wrote that Book."

I answered, "I do know it for a fact."

He retorted, "There are no facts."

I asked him, "Is this airplane flying?"

He answered, "I don't know."

The pilot had in fact just a few moments earlier spoken over the loudspeaker, telling us that we were flying at 35,000 feet and at a speed of 560 miles per hour.

So I asked the young college man again, "Is this airplane flying?"

"I'm not sure," he replied.

I then asked him a third time, "Is this airplane flying?"

This time he replied, "I think it is." I then turned to the businessman and asked him the same question.

You will find this hard to believe, but he also said, "I don't know."

By this time, most of the people on the plane were listening to our conversation, so I turned to the man across the aisle and, with a very loud and emphatic voice, I asked him, "Sir, do you know if this plane is flying or not?"

He stood up and said to the entire plane, "Let me be the first to say, this airplane is flying."

I then turned to the businessman and college student and said, "This airplane is flying, and that is a fact."

The young man looked at me and said, "Okay, Sir, I concede that it is a fact that this airplane is flying."

I said, "Thank you very much." I lifted my Bible into the air and as loudly as I could, I said, "Since there's one fact, there are two: GOD wrote this Book."

To understand the ignorance of this world, you have to realize when he said there are no facts, that he was saying it was a fact that there were no facts. When I departed from the plane, you could have driven a D-9 caterpillar in front of me and hit no one. It was like the parting of the Red Sea as people gave me plenty of space, but I praise the Lord for the boldness He gave me to stand up for His name.

I suppose it would be good to tell you how the Lord persuaded me that I was to begin flying to my meetings. For the first four years that I was an evangelist, I drove, took a bus, or rode a train to all my meetings because I didn't care anything about flying. During those years, however, the Lord had been speaking to me about flying, and I had been refusing. I was driving toward San Francisco, California, on a four-lane highway where I was going to preach a revival meeting when I unexpectedly met a car coming at me head on. The driver was driving the wrong way, and we were both running the speed limit, which at that time was 70 mph. I knew it wasn't going to be long before we collided with each other, and seeing that he was going to hit me head on, I spun the wheel of my car to the right. He hit me at the post of the driver's door, catapulting my car into the air with such force that my car spiraled several times in the air before landing on the ground. The highway department had planted sponge-like bushes which were very thick along this particular part of the highway, and my car landed on these spongy bushes. Though my car landed upside down, I was not hurt, and I was able to unfasten my seat belt and crawl out of the car through the window. A number of cars stopped, and people came running up to me, terrified that I was surely dead. However, I was able to tell them I was fine; and having a pocket full of tracts, I was also able to share Christ with many of them.

The Lord again spoke to my heart and said, "Tom, are you going to fly or do you want Me to get really tough?"

I said with a smile, "Father, I am on my way to the airport." I flew home from that meeting in San Francisco to Southern California where we were living at that time and continued to fly for the next 40 years as I have already mentioned, some five million miles.

On another flight, this time flying into Des Moines, Iowa, we were at 5,000 feet when the pilot came on over the loudspeaker and said, "Hold on, buckle up, we are going in for an emergency landing." Of course, none of us on the plane knew for what reason; so needless to say, many anxious people were wondering what had happened. In a few minutes as we landed and rolled to a stop, the pilot came on the speaker again and said, "I really apologize, ladies and gentlemen, but I have a 30-to 35-pound goose lying in my lap because it came right through the windshield." I am told by some airline pilots that they have actually seen Canada geese flying as high as 35,000 feet.

⁂

One day while we were living in Murfreesboro, Tennessee, a young man who was working part-time for the ministry drove us to the airport. During the 30-minute drive, I pulled off my suit coat as I dictated some letters to be taken back for my secretary to type. He dropped us off at the curb where we checked in our luggage then said our goodbyes. Pam, her caregiver at the time, Pam Alcorn, and I began walking to our departure gate. We were nearly at the gate when I suddenly realized I didn't have my suit coat. I am not in the regular practice of pulling off my suit coat and do not know why I did so that morning, but there I was without it. I told the ladies to go on to the gate, and I went back to the curb of the airport.

As I walked back to the curb, I prayed, "Heavenly Father, You know my driver is halfway back to Murfreesboro by now, but I need that suit coat. Please ask him to turn around, look in the back seat, see my suit coat, and then return to the airport." I stood outside at the curbside waiting for my coat to be returned to me when the skycap who checked us in walked over to me and asked, "Mr. Williams, is everything okay? Didn't I check you in correctly?"

"Yes, you checked us in fine," I told him, "but I left my suit coat in the back seat of the car."

The skycap said, "Well, Sir, your driver must be halfway back to Murfreesboro by now."

"Yes, I know, but I just asked God to show him my coat and bring it back here to me," I answered the skycap.

He gave me a sidelong, unbelieving look, and then said, "Uh, you don't mind if I wait here with you, do you? I got to see this."

I laughed, clapped him on the back, and said, "I don't mind at

~ 114 ~

all." A few moments later my car came into view as it rounded the corner and came to a stop by us at the curb.

My driver got out of the car and said, "Have you been praying? About halfway back to Murfreesboro, God told me to turn and look in the back seat. When I did, I saw your coat and knew you would need it, so I turned around and came back."

"Well, I did ask God to tell you to turn around and look in the car's back seat. Thanks," I replied.

The skycap said, "Wow! God did just what you said He would."

"Yes," I answered, "God is great to answer prayer." I did not have a problem after that to get that skycap to believe that prayer really works. I know all kinds of Christians who don't mind praying if they don't "have to go to the curb."

I had changed planes in Salt Lake City one night and boarded a flight to Bozeman, Montana, where we were living at the time, when I noticed some fluid coming out of the right wing as we were taxiing down the runway. I got the attention of one of the stewardesses, pointed out the problem, and said, "I don't think that should be happening." She immediately went and told the pilot who instantly shut down the plane.

The leaking fluid turned out to be the hydraulic fluid, the loss of which would have left the plane basically uncontrollable. The pilot called for a tow vehicle, and the plane was pulled back to the gate. We were told we would be boarding a new airplane that the company had just purchased. Of course, we were all so thankful that the problem had been detected and that we would be flying home on a new plane; however, the plane was so new that the pilot did not know how to start it. This inability did not do anything to build our confidence that had already been shaken. They sent for a mechanic who had recently gone to school to learn about this new aircraft. He came and started the airplane, then rode to Bozeman with us for which we were all thankful. I was able to speak to the pilot and copilot as we deplaned in Bozeman about the goodness of God in making the fluid leak before we were in the air. They both consented that it was God's protection as I handed them both Gospel tracts and was able to lead them to the Saviour.

God worked another wonderful miracle for my family and me a couple of years following Pam's illness. We had been able to sell the Grinstead's motor home and eventually the Criswell's motor home, which helped our finances; however, the payments on our motor home were still a constant financial strain. With needing to alleviate the constant financial pressure and knowing the stability of a home would be better both for the children and Pam, I put the motor home up for sale and sought to find a home. I was able to find a house to rent in the Denver, Colorado, area and moved my family out of the motor home.

The move didn't take long because all we had were five sleeping bags, one chair, some dishes, some tableware, and our clothes. We had no money to purchase the items we needed.

Two weeks after we moved, God answered our prayers and sent a miracle when He arranged for a businessman and me to meet. I told this man about our situation, and with enthusiasm he said, "Praise the Lord! I'm glad God chose me to meet your needs."

The next day this gentleman took me to the furniture store and bought furniture for every room in our house. He also purchased a new refrigerator as well as a washer and a dryer for our family. That same week his wife came and chose bedspreads for each bedroom and hung matching drapes. The Lord had truly done exceedingly, abundantly above what we had asked or thought.

One of the ladies who helped to care for my wife had heard me tell many stories of God's amazing answers to prayer. She said, "I want to see one of these answers. I want you to pray and ask God to provide the next tank of gas we will need." At the time of her request, we were in Inglewood, Florida, and traveling to Ft. Myers, Florida. When we started out of Inglewood, the gas tank gauge was registering near the empty mark. I had been much in prayer for this request the night before, so I asked my Heavenly Father which station He wanted me to pull into for gas, and He replied, "The very next one." As we pulled into the station, the lady asked, "You're going to fill up here? You're not going to pay for it, right?"

"No, I'm not going to pay for it," I told her. When I put the hose in the tank to fill it up, the Devil said, "God didn't do it, did He?"

I replied, "The tank isn't full yet."

At that point the station attendant walked to my car and said, "You must be Tom Williams. I was told by a gentleman who came in earlier that a cowboy named Tom Williams would be stopping here, and he left the money to pay for your gas." When the tank was full, the attendant said, "I'll get your change," which was nearly $20.

We have a fish pond in our front yard where we live now, and one day the circulating pump which moves the water over a small waterfall stopped working. The man who was working for us at the time came to me and said, "I have done everything that I know, and the pump just will not work."

I knew that we did not need to spend the money on a new pump, so I asked him, "Have you prayed about it?"

He replied, "Honestly, I have not."

"Well, let's bow our heads and pray," I said. When we finished praying, I told him to start the pump, which he did, and the water immediately began pouring over the waterfall.

PRAYER AND FAITH:

The Life of Dr. Tom Williams

He asked me, "What is the difference between a prayer *time* and a prayer *life?*"

I answered, "When I asked you to fix the pump, you tried everything except prayer; the only thing that I tried was prayer."

He smiled and said, "I understand, Dr. Williams."

A similar situation occurred with one of our riding lawn mowers; I was told that it wouldn't start. Two different men had tried to start the lawn mower and sought to figure out what the difficulty was—without success. Once we had returned to the ranch and knowing that the grass needed mowing, I sat down on the lawn mower and prayed, "Heavenly Father, You know we need to mow the grass. Please make the lawn mower start." The lawn mower started without difficulty and has continued to work ever since I prayed. Not only was it an answer to prayer, but it was also a testimony to these men of the power of God to answer prayer.

The Scriptures teach us to pray about everything: yet, it has been my experience that most people do not take that admonition seriously. All through our ministry, I have sought the Lord in prayer first, whether it is to repair household items, to repair equipment, to provide parking places, to provide seats on the airplanes, or to provide in any other what would be termed mundane and ordinary situations. I am so thankful for the great truth in Philippians 4:6 and what it has meant to me. That verse has taught me to pray about everything without exception. I challenge you to read, memorize, and live by this verse which says, *"Be careful for nothing; but in every thing by prayer and supplication with thanksgiving let your requests be made known unto God."*

CHAPTER NINE

God's Amazing Salvation

I WAS PREACHING IN BUFFALO, NEW YORK, when the Lord saved a man and his wife and turned them from selling liquor to sharing Christ with lost souls. This couple had just started attending the church, and the pastor asked me to be very careful about saying anything against liquor. I knew of a certainty that God wanted me to preach against liquor and the sale of it, so not wanting to hinder the Spirit, I did preach the sermon against liquor. That man and his wife did not come back for three nights, but on the fourth night they returned. When I finished preaching, both the man and his wife came running down the aisle during the invitation. He said, "I have not slept since I was here the other day. We need to be saved, and tomorrow my liquor stores will be put up for sale." The couple joined the church, began to be very faithful in their attendance, and became some of the greatest servants that the church ever had.

A teenager from this same church in New York asked me to pray for his father who was a drunk. He asked me if I would go with him to meet his dad and share Christ with him, which I readily agreed to do. This young man took me to the bar where his dad spent much of his time and introduced me to him. I asked the man if he would come and hear me preach just once. He agreed to come on Sunday morning; however, following Sunday school, the man's son came to me and said, "My dad is not coming this morning."

I told the young man, "Your dad may lie to some people, but he isn't going to lie to me." I asked the preacher to start the service and told him I would be back in time to preach. The boy and I arrived at his home, and I asked the boy's mother, "Where is your husband?"

"He is in bed asleep," she answered. After asking her where the bedroom was, I proceeded to march down the hall, enter the bedroom, and wake him up. I said to him, "You promised me you would be in church this morning, and you are going."

His answer to me was, "I don't want to go." I told him again that he had promised and that he was going to go to church. He got out of bed, got dressed, and rode to church with his son and me. We arrived just in time for me to preach the morning service, and though he was attentive, he did not get saved. As he left the church, I told him I was going to pray every day that God would save his soul. I was at the church for several days, but he never came back again.

When I was finished with the meetings, I went to another church 90 miles south to hold revival meetings. One night during these meetings, I saw that man sitting in one of the pews. I preached my heart out, but he did not get saved. That meeting closed on a Sunday evening, and the pastor drove me 90 miles to the same airport that I had flown into where I was to catch a red-eye flight at 12:15 a.m. When we arrived at the airport, I only had a few minutes to get my ticket and board the plane, so I rushed to the ticket counter and said, "I have to be on the 12:15 a.m. flight."

The ticket agent said, "Okay, but take it easy. The flight is an hour and a half late because there is a heavy fog in Florida, which is delaying your plane from getting here."

Once I was handed my ticket for the flight, I walked around the podium to take a seat in the waiting area. There in one of the seats was that young teenager's father. He stood up, greeted me, and said, "Preacher, I couldn't sleep, and my son told me you were flying out of here tonight." With tears slipping down his face, he said, "I need to be saved." There in the airport we knelt, and he received the Lord Jesus Christ as his Saviour. The Lord had fogged in Florida so I would have time to show this man how to be saved. What a mighty God we serve!

God wonderfully saved another gentleman in one of my meetings. He was the vice-president for one of the largest trucking companies in America, and he had professed to be a Christian. One night during the invitation, he came forward for salvation and went home that night knowing the Lord and the Lord's knowing him. He attended each service during that revival meeting and following the second night he said, "I have a large bar in my house. What should I do now that I'm saved?"

I answered, "You need to throw it all away and completely sell out to the Lord."

He had thousands of dollars of the finest liquor in the world but brought it all to church in big boxes the next night. For a long time he, the pastor, and I opened all those bottles and poured their contents down the sink of the church. He said, "Now, I want you to come to work with me tomorrow so you can watch me and tell me if I am a good witness for the Lord."

I went to work with him the next day, and he put me in a corner of his very large personal office so I could observe and listen as he dealt with prospective customers. The president of a large truck manufacturing corporation was the first to come into his office that day. This man asked the president of the corporation, "What are you doing tonight?"

The president answered, "Not a thing in the world."

"Then I want you to go to church with me," he told him.

I am sure that man thought he was going to be invited to a wild party, but when the invitation to go to church was posed to him, he began to make excuses and said, "Well, I do have to catch a flight tonight."

"Okay, then let's just forget those 50 trucks I ordered this week," the vice-president stated. (I had to suppress a chuckle at the way this man was seeking to get folks to come to church, but truthfully, I was quite proud of the sincerity with which it was done.)

The man's response was, "Well, maybe I could go with you to church tonight."

The second man to have an appointment was a vice-president of a large truck motor manufacturing company. He also invited this man to attend church with him that night and received the same type of response that he had with the first gentleman. "We will just cancel that order for 60 truck engines that we tentatively made last week," was the answer given to this second man.

When the vice-president left his office, he too had finally agreed to attend church with him that night. These types of conversations went on all day long, and at the end of the day, he said to me, "How am I doing, Tom?"

I said with a chuckle, "Believe me, you are doing great."

In the revival service that night several presidents and vice-presidents of corporations across America were in attendance. Though none of those men who came to the service that night received Christ, this gentleman who brought them continued to be a witness for the Lord—even after becoming president of one of the largest commercial van corporations in the world. Following his retirement, he went to teach in a fundamental Bible college for several years before being called to his eternal reward in Heaven.

In the late 1960s, I had been in Los Angeles holding meetings and was on my way to the airport to catch a plane home to

Colorado. Due to the Los Angeles traffic being heavier that day, I missed my flight by five minutes, though I made a gallant effort to run to the boarding gate once I arrived at the airport. The door had already been closed, and the plane was pulling away from the gate. I watched with a heavy heart as the plane taxied out to the runway and took off without me. I so wanted to be on it as I had been away from home for a couple of weeks. As I watched it fly out of sight, I said, "Heavenly Father, You must have a tremendous reason for me to miss my flight."

About that time a little boy with a shoeshine box walked up and asked me if I would like my boots shined.

I said, "You must be the reason why I just missed my flight home."

"No, Sir," he said, "I didn't have a thing to do with it."

I said, "Yes, I think you did, and I'm going to tell you why while you shine my boots." I told him about the Lord Jesus Christ's coming from Heaven and being born in a manger. I told him how that little baby grew up, became a man, was sinless, and as a result, He could and did die for our sins. I continued, "Today He wanted me to tell you this story so that you could be saved and go to Heaven. Would you like to ask the Lord Jesus Christ to be your Saviour?"

The little shoeshine boy answered, "Can I be saved here in the airport?"

I said, "You can be saved right here by this shoeshine box. Would you like to kneel right here and ask the Lord to save you?"

He answered, "I sure would."

I'm sure many folks thought this was a strange sight—he and I knelt by his little shoeshine box, and he asked the Lord to save him. Just as soon as he had prayed and confessed Christ as his Saviour, he jumped up, stuck everything in his shine box, and started running.

"Where are you going?" I asked. "I haven't paid you yet."

He stopped for a moment and said, "Mister, I'm going to tell my momma that I just asked Jesus to be my Saviour. She has wanted me to do that for a long time. She is going to be so happy." It is amazing what God will do and how God will use us to reach a precious soul for Him.

~❧~

A number of years ago at a revival meeting in the Midwest, a lady remained in her pew though the service had been dismissed and everyone except the pastor, his family, and I had gone home. Noticing that she continued to sit there in the pew, I walked up to her and said, "Would you like to be saved?"

She replied, "Don't mock me, Preacher."

I said, "Ma'am, I'm not mocking you," then asked her again, "Wouldn't you like to be saved?"

She again replied, "Don't mock me, Preacher." I assured her once more that I was not in any way mocking her, and she said, "You don't know what I do or who I am. God will not save someone like me."

I said, "Ma'am, it doesn't matter who you are or what you do, the Lord will save you through His Son, Jesus Christ."

She said, "I am a go-go girl, and after my work every night, I sell my body to men." At that point she began to weep, and as the tears made their way through the heavy makeup, she finally looked up at me and said with a broken heart, "Preacher, will God *really* save me?"

I looked at her and replied, "He specializes in saving those who are so far from Him." In my heart I could not help but think of the wondrous transformation He made in the life of Mary Magdalene. I said, "We can kneel down right here, and you can call on the Lord to save you." As she knelt down at her pew, she began to pour out her heart to the Lord, and 30 minutes later when she felt that she had confessed everything to God, she lifted her eyes toward Heaven and said, "If You have salvation for someone like me, I receive right now the Lord Jesus Christ as my Saviour." The transformation that God did in her heart that night was evident on her face as she stood to her feet, and she made her way out the door to her car after jubilantly telling the pastor and his family that she had received Christ as her Saviour.

The pastor and I were sitting on the platform before the service started the next night when we noticed this same lady, now nicely dressed, walking down the aisle with two little boys about five and six years old and her husband, a man well over six feet tall. They marched right up onto the platform and stopped immediately in front of the pastor and me. She looked at me, smiled, and said, "Do you remember me?"

I replied with a hearty, "Yes, Ma'am, but you look so much better and different tonight."

She said, "Preacher, I went home last night for the first time in over six months. I had no idea what kind of reception I would receive, but with much fear and trembling, I knocked on the front door, then got down on my knees. When my husband opened the door, I reached out and put my arms around his legs just above his feet and asked if he could ever receive me back again. He told me he knew where I had been and what I had been doing and that he and the boys were wondering when I would come home. He then reached down very tenderly, picked me up, and drew me to himself in such a loving embrace. God is really good, isn't He?"

I answered her, "Yes, He really is."

It is wonderful to know that God is no respecter of persons, that He will save any who come to Him, regardless of their walk of life. Just as He saved the lady with such a background as the one I have just mentioned, He wonderfully saved a lady from the other end of the spectrum while I was preaching in the Northwest.

PRAYER AND FAITH:
The Life of Dr. Tom Williams

Following the service one night, a lady walked up to me and said, "I heard you speak on the radio today, so I came out to see what you were like." It was obvious that she was a very wealthy woman by the way she was dressed. She continued, "Could you prove to me that there is a God?"

I suppose she was expecting me to go into a dissertation on the subject of Creation or perhaps a lengthy reasoning from scientific proof of some kind that evolution could not possibly be true. I didn't choose either one. Instead, I stepped back, took hold of both sides of my suit coat, opened my suit coat, and said, "Take a look."

She looked at me quite bewildered and said, "Are you God?"

"No, Ma'am," I replied, "I'm a modern-day miracle." I explained to her that when God saved me, I was a drinker and a smoker, was an extremely filthy talker, was as addicted to country and western music as young people are to rock 'n' roll today, and was as ungodly as a man could be. I related to her my salvation experience and told her it was not a *reformation* nor *rehabilitation*, but a miracle of *regeneration*. I said, "It did not take God five years, five months, five weeks, five hours nor even five minutes till He made me a new creature in Christ, and then two weeks later He called me to preach!"

She then said, "Tell me more about this salvation and about your Saviour." After 45 minutes of explaining salvation to her, she said, "I would like to be saved."

"Wonderful," I said, "let's walk down to the front of the church where we can kneel at the altar and you can call on the Lord to save you."

I'm sure what happened next was very amusing to the pastor and the few people who still remained in the church building. Upon reaching the altar, I immediately knelt down and waited for her to kneel; however, she did not kneel down. I looked at her and stated, "You need to kneel down."

She asked, "Do you have to kneel to be saved? I'm sure you must recognize by my jewelry and my clothes that I'm a very wealthy person."

I replied, "Yes, Ma'am, it is evident that you have money."

She said, "The society circles that I am connected with do not do such things."

I stood up and I said, "Okay, perhaps you can come back tomorrow night."

"No, I want to be saved," she said. "I might not live till tomorrow night."

I said, "Okay, let's kneel down." I got back on my knees, waited for her, and she still did not kneel.

She asked me again, "Do you have to kneel to be saved?"

I answered, "No, most people do not have to kneel, but you are one who must kneel before the Lord because you have so much pride in who you are and in what you possess that we have to find a way to get rid of that pride." I then stood up again and said, "Perhaps tomorrow night you could come again."

Once again she said, "No, I want to be saved tonight."

I returned to my knees, and this lady sincerely tried to kneel. She came about halfway down to kneeling and then stood straight up as if something had hit her. She looked at the altar like she thought it might bite her; however, she did make a second attempt at kneeling—still without success.

I don't know if any of you have ever watched a cow lie down, but they do it a little differently than most other creatures. First, their front end goes down halfway, making them appear as if they are bowing, then part of their back end descends. Finally, they collapse a little more in the front and then in the back, suddenly dropping full force to the ground. Though I did not time it, I think the third time this lady started to kneel, it must have taken her a full minute before her knees hit the carpet. When her knees finally touched the carpet, every drop of pride in her was gone, and the floodgates of her soul broke open as tears unashamedly fell down her face as she cried out to the God of Heaven to save her. She went home that night rejoicing in the Lord.

As I sat on the platform the next night, it was a blessing to see her walk through the doors with her 20-year-old daughter who came to the Saviour at the close of the service. Some months later I received a letter from her telling me they were both going to Bible college because they wanted to learn all they could about the Lord Who had saved them.

A young high school girl with tears flowing down her face walked the aisle for salvation during a revival meeting I was preaching in Northern California. After the service that night, she came to the pastor and me and asked, "What can I do to show my high school classmates what happened to me tonight?"

I told her, "I want you to take my Bible, explaining to her that I had another one in my hotel room, and I want you to put the Bible on top of your school books and carry it there all day."

The very next night she came back to the meeting and, before the service ever started, came and said to me, "It was a bad day at school." I asked her what had happened, and she said, "Brother Williams, my mom and dad own a bar in this town. I have always had the liberty to do just about everything that I wanted to do. They have not cared who I have dated or what time of night I came home. I have had relations with some boys in my school. When they saw the Bible on top of my books, they began to taunt me." She shared that they had made comments like, "Is that Bible going to make you a good girl? Remember us? We're the boys that know you."

She told me the boys just made fun of her and laughed about the

Bible. She said, "It was an extremely bad day at school. What am I to do now, Preacher?"

I told her, "Tomorrow you again take the Bible and put it on top of your books. When you see those boys, tell them they're right. Say, 'What I did with you was sin, but ever since the other night, I am whiter than snow because I have been washed in the blood of the Lamb.'"

As you read this book, let me ask you, do **you** really believe that she is whiter than snow?

You may say, "Yes, I believe that."

Then I have one other question, "Can she marry your son?" You see, God's salvation really is great; for it took Rahab the harlot, washed her clean, and put her in the lineage of our Lord Jesus Christ.

⁓

I was preaching in a church in Arizona when the Lord's mighty hand of salvation reached down and snatched another lost soul from the fiery flames of Hell. I was introduced to a man I was told was one of the most faithful and hardworking men of the church. This man asked me to pray for his wife to be saved. He said, "She will come to church with me once in a great while when we are having a special preacher. I would like you to pray with me that she will come to church one night this week." The Lord answered our prayer, and on the last night of the meeting, his wife walked into the church building with him. That night the Lord moved upon my heart and led me to share the story of Pam's illness and how God had enabled me to care for her.

When I gave the invitation to come and be saved, this man's wife was the first one down the aisle, and she said, "Many of America's greatest preachers have been in this church, yet I was always able to say 'no' to all of their preaching and pleading for souls to be saved. But tonight as I sat and listened, for the first time I saw the love of God flow through a man in caring for His wife. I know now what the verse means that '*God so loved the world, that he gave his only begotten Son, that whosoever believeth in him should not perish, but have everlasting life.*' With that kind of love, I must receive Jesus Christ as my Saviour." Needless to say, her husband was overwhelmed with joy, and the entire church was thrilled with what God had done.

Several weeks later I was preaching a large banquet in Los Angeles, California, to raise money for a skid-row mission and noticed this same man and his wife had driven from Phoenix to be in the meeting. She said, "If you would have told me a few weeks ago that I would be saved and that I would drive all this distance to hear you preach again, I would have thought you were crazy."

I replied, "Yes, it is wonderful that God's amazing salvation makes us new creatures."

∽◡◠

Early in my ministry before God had called me to be an evangelist, I preached each weekend at a little church in the town of Temecula, California, which was about 100 miles east of Los Angeles. On one particular Saturday, I was at the church in Temecula getting some addresses so I could go calling on the new visitors. On this same day, a man in an expensive sports car drove into the church parking lot needing directions, as he had taken a wrong turn and was lost. While I was telling him how to get back to the road he needed to be on, the Spirit of God spoke to my heart that this man was lost in two ways. I began to tell him how he could know the Lord Jesus Christ as his Saviour. He began to weep as I told him of the great love the Saviour had for lost souls such as himself. He told me that he had left Los Angeles that morning aimlessly driving, not caring where he went. He said, "I just had to go somewhere and try to get my thoughts together. In the last few days, unknown to my wife, I have gambled away all of our savings and equity in our home. I simply cannot face her and the children with what I have done."

I told him that I agreed that what he had done was very selfish and very wicked but that God would save him, and through the blood of the Lord Jesus Christ, his sins would be forgiven. After spending some time taking him through the Scriptures, he bowed his head and received the Lord Jesus Christ as his Saviour. He asked me if it would be possible for me to visit his home and speak to his wife and children about the sin he had committed and about how he had gotten saved. He also wanted me to explain to them how they also could be saved. I told him I would come to his house on the following Monday night to visit him and his family. Throughout the entire weekend, I fervently prayed that God would help his wife and children to forgive him and, at the same time, the Lord would open their hearts to salvation. My Heavenly Father heard and answered my prayers in a wonderful way. His wife knew that he was addicted to gambling and was so thrilled that he had repented and had been saved. She freely forgave him, and so did the children. They all received Jesus Christ as their Saviour, and God had worked another tremendous miracle by bringing an entire family unto Himself.

I remember a day when God used a rock slide to facilitate an opportunity to share Christ with a number of 18-wheel truck drivers. The rock slide had caused all travel along the Interstate to cease, and vehicles were parked as far back along the road as the eye could see. As we were sitting in the motor home waiting for the Interstate to be cleared of rock and debris, we heard over the CB one of the truck drivers who was caught in the same delay begin to swear about the situation. I jumped up and speaking on the CB said, "Don't be cussing on this channel! I'm a preacher, and besides that, God is listening."

He answered back and said, "God is not listening."

I replied, "He hears every word you say wherever you are." Then one truck driver after another spoke to him saying comments like, "Shut your mouth. Truck drivers have bad enough reputations without your help!"

Finally he said, "Okay, okay, I'm sorry. I wouldn't be like this if I just had a cup of coffee."

I asked, "What kind of truck are you driving?"

He described his truck to me, and looking in my rearview mirror, I saw him about 15 vehicles behind our motor home. I said, "I'm in this big motor home up here in front of you; I'll put on a pot of coffee and bring you some in a few minutes."

He sarcastically answered, "Yes, I bet you will."

"You hold on," I said, "and I'll be there."

After we made a pot of coffee, I took the coffee, cups, a case of candy bars a church had given us, and a pocket full of tracts and walked between the long rows of vehicles to his truck. I gave him a cup of coffee, a candy bar, and a tract and told him about the Lord. I poured coffee, gave out candy bars, and shared Jesus Christ with truck driver after truck driver during the many hours we were delayed in the middle of the Interstate.

I was also given the opportunity to talk to a highway patrol officer about the Lord and jokingly told him, "Witnessing to you is putting law under grace!" We had a good laugh together while he enjoyed a cup of coffee and eagerly took a tract about the Saviour.

During the four and one half hours we were delayed on that Interstate, I was privileged to watch several men bow their heads and unashamedly receive the Lord Jesus Christ as their Saviour. God taught me a great lesson that day about allowing Him to direct the events and circumstances in our daily lives.

I had asked Him at the beginning of the day to lead us and to

help us to do His will, but as we came upon the rock slide and traffic jam, I began to inwardly complain because I had many miles to
cover to arrive at our destination on time. God wonderfully reminded me of my prayer that morning, and I was able to see His will in
the rock slide and be used to bring souls to Christ. Many of us, like
I initially did that morning, want His will *if* it coincides with what we
have planned; however, He will do abundantly above what we ask or
think if we completely commit ourselves to Him in everything—
even a rock slide. The Interstate was finally cleared, allowing the
long line of vehicles to move again; and the next 200 miles we continued to hear truck drivers who were caught in the rock slide delay
tell other truck drivers traveling the opposite way, "You missed it
today! We had an old-fashioned revival meeting during a delay
because of a rock slide. A preacher carried coffee, candy, and the
story of Jesus to all of us."

Only Heaven will reveal what the Lord did that day in so many
hearts.

The Lord uses people, circumstances, and various events to
bring lost souls to Christ. The way in which He does this isn't always
how we would choose, but as the Bible says in Isaiah 55:8, 9, "...*my
thoughts are not your thoughts, neither are your ways my ways, saith the
LORD. For as the heavens are higher than the earth, so are my ways higher than your ways, and my thoughts than your thoughts.*" Our ways are
not His ways because His ways are much higher than ours.

Pam faithfully prayed many years for the salvation of her friend's
husband, and it seemed that nothing would reach this man to turn
his heart to Christ. Soon after Pam's illness, I took her prayer list,
which she kept in a small notebook, showed it to him and then
reminded him that Pam had prayed so faithfully all these years for
him. God answered Pam's prayer that day, and with a broken heart

and yielded spirit, he received Christ as his Saviour. Both he and his wife visited Pam while she was in the hospital, and as they stood beside her bed, he said, "Nothing else has ever touched my heart as knowing you prayed so faithfully for me. Thank you for being willing to be in a coma that I might be saved."

CHAPTER TEN

≈≈

The Storm of Our Life

IN FEBRUARY OF 1978, DURING OUR eighteenth year of our marriage, a storm came to our family that only the grace of God could calm and sustain. Pam and I had agreed to co-host a group on a ten-day tour of Israel with a pastor and his wife from Maryland. Our group consisted of 55 people from churches across America with our son Tim, now 22 years old, being one of them. After flying all night, our plane landed in Jordan. Though we were subdued by the presence of the armed guards surrounding our plane, it did not completely dampen our group's excitement and enthusiasm.

Our tour began in the city of Petra, which is sometimes referred to as "the Rose Red City of the Dead." Many years ago it was thought by some that Israel would flee to Petra during times of persecution as the city is carved into the walls of the great red cliffs in that country. As we left Jordan and crossed into Israel, we experienced what it is like to be thoroughly searched. The female guards took each lady and even searched meticulously through her hair. The heels of my cowboy boots were x-rayed. The guards even cut the tops out of several of the briefcases businessmen in our group were carrying. Those with a camera were required to take a picture of themselves to insure the camera was not some type of weapon. Our luggage was opened, and our clothing was carefully inspected.

I must wonder—have we, as King David did in Psalm 139:23, ever asked the Lord to search our hearts, knowing the search will be even more thorough and meticulous than it was for our entering Israel? *"Search me, O God, and know my heart: try me, and know my thoughts."* That was an experience I have never forgotten.

Once we were granted entry into Israel, we boarded the tour buses, which took us to see many Biblical sights such as Gideon's stream, Mt. Carmel, the ruins of Capernaum, and the cliffs where the pigs ran over the side into the Sea of Galilee. At the Sea of Galilee, we journeyed to the other side in a boat that was much like the one the Lord and His disciples used. While on the sea, Brother Grinstead inspired our thoughts by singing "Master, the Tempest Is Raging" and thrilled our hearts when he sang "Stranger of Galilee" as we neared the shore. At other places along our tour, Brother Grinstead sang such soul-stirring songs like "Fill My Cup, Lord" while at Jacob's well and "The Old Rugged Cross" during our visit to the garden tomb.

It was at the end of our tour while at Mt. Masada that the storm blew unexpectedly and fiercely into our lives. We were on the tram traveling up to the top of Mt. Masada when quite suddenly Pam's entire body began to tremble and shake. I took her in my arms and asked, "What is the matter?"

She replied, "I don't know; I can't stop this shaking."

"Have you been hurting and haven't told me?"

She assured me she had not, and what was happening was as strange to her as it was to me. When the tram stopped, I picked her up in my arms and carried her up the steps that led to the top of the mountain. I laid her down on a nearby bench and put her head in my lap while the rest of the group toured Mt. Masada. I covered her with my own coat and a number of other coats belonging to members of our group, trying to keep her warm and hopefully stop the shaking. However, the shaking and trembling only seemed to continually increase.

With the help of Tim, Mrs. Grinstead, and some of the other men from our group, we assisted Pam down the very steep trail off of Masada. In those days the tour buses drove the groups to the tram station and then drove around the mountain while the groups toured Masada, and picked them up on the other side. For this reason, we had to walk down this trail.

When we met the bus, I asked our guide to speak to the driver and tell him that my wife was very sick and needed to be taken to a hospital. We were driven to an army encampment where, with the help of the guide, we were able to persuade the army of Israel to loan us an ambulance to rush my wife to Beersheba, Israel. I rode the 75 miles with Pam to Beersheba and admitted her to the army hospital where the doctors worked on Pam for several hours, yet were unable to determine what was wrong with her. They told me they could not make a diagnosis because Pam had not been sick long enough for the disease to develop. With urgency they said to me, "You need to get your wife back to America as soon as possible. Your country has the best medical facilities in the world."

The tour bus had since driven the group to Tel Aviv, and I needed to catch a taxi cab to meet them at the airport. However, the language barrier was making it difficult for the taxi driver to fully understand what I needed. God, in His mercy, provided a young lady from the hospital waiting lounge to interpret, and soon Pam and I were on our way to Tel Aviv.

At the airport Pam and I had some trouble getting through customs due to her illness, but once I told them the doctors recommended I take her to the States as soon as possible, we were granted clearance, and we boarded the plane.

The airline was very gracious to us and arranged for us to occupy an entire row of seats so Pam could lie down with her head in my lap. When we landed at the JFK Airport in New York, we once again had difficulty getting through customs, but the Lord intervened. We were finally cleared and allowed to board our final flight which would take us to the National Airport in Washington, D.C., where our other three children were waiting for our return. Arriving at our final destination, Pam wanted to go to the motor home rather than a hospital, so we went straight to the motor home so she could lie down.

Shortly after arriving at our motor home, it was apparent Pam was not getting better, and I insisted we go to the hospital. The pastor of the church where our motor home was parked very graciously drove us to the nearby hospital in Alexandria, Virginia. There Pam was admitted and taken to a room where the doctors began to run tests, seeking to diagnose Pam's illness.

As the night progressed, so did Pam's level of pain; in fact, her pain was so intense she was hitting and kicking the bed rails. The doctors felt the need to bind her hands and feet so she could not injure herself. By this time she had lost all ability to speak, and the doctors said to me, "We believe that your wife is mentally ill, and we can do nothing else until she has been examined by a psychiatrist."

I firmly replied, "You may call a psychiatrist, but my wife will not be put in a mental ward. Her illness is not mental."

The psychiatrist was called, but he did not get to Pam's room until an hour later. Though I was fearful of the outcome, it soon became apparent he was God sent. Pam was still able to shake her head "yes" or "no" in answer to the three questions the psychiatrist asked her. After the third question, the psychiatrist looked at the two physicians and said, "It's not mental; it's physical, and you better do something quick."

A Chinese man, an internal disease specialist who had been called in on Pam's case, stepped forward and told me he would be my wife's doctor. He asked me to immediately sign a release for a lower lumbar puncture, which I did as Pam was being rolled away to have this procedure performed. I did not know it would be the last time I would see her as the Pam to whom I had been married for the last 18 years.

After the lower lumbar puncture, the doctor explained to me that my wife had bacterial meningitis, and the type of meningitis she had was a double multiplication germ. He added, "Her spinal pressure was extremely high, and to test it again would perhaps collapse the spinal column."

The fluid in the spinal column is normally the consistency of water; however, Pam's was the consistency of buttermilk. During his explanation of the disease, he then said as kindly as possible, "Your wife will probably be dead in less than 24 hours as she has lapsed into a coma with seizures and convulsions, and her temperature has spiked to 108°."

The severity of the situation was overwhelming, and the enormity of what I had just heard took my breath away. Still, I had to know everything was being done for Pam that could be done, so I asked him if there was anything that could possibly help her.

He said, "The germ responds to penicillin, but the doses would have to be so large that it would probably kill your wife. I really do not believe anything will help at this point."

With that barest glimmer of hope, I said, "Let's give it a try; it seems to me that we have nothing to lose."

I signed a release form, and he administered 24 million units of penicillin to Pam, which was repeated in 12 hours. Then she received 24 million units a day for the next 12 days. Once I had signed the release form, I went to the hospital chapel, dropped to my knees, bowed my head, and told the Lord the same thing I had told Him when Wanda was in the throes of death. "If You want to take Pam Home, I will understand." I also told Him, "If You are going to take Pam home, please let her go quickly that she might not go through a tremendous amount of suffering."

Pam remained in the intensive care unit for two weeks; then I was told they were going to take Pam out of ICU and put her in acute care. They did not believe Pam was going to live as further tests revealed her brain was completely dead. They wanted the family to be able to be with her as much as possible.

The doctors were convinced Pam could not live, so they would not perform any kind of physical therapy nor put weights on her arms and legs to keep them from atrophying. However, I daily massaged her arms and legs, believing God for a miracle. After several weeks of watching her deteriorate, I said to the doctor, "I'd like to take my wife to our hometown in Denver, Colorado."

I needed to put our children in a Christian school as Pam had been homeschooling them during the three years of our traveling in the motor homes. The doctor asked me how I would be transporting her, and I said, "In our motor home."

He said, "You just can't do that. Your wife cannot make that kind of journey."

I called the airlines to arrange something with them, but they wanted me to rent one section of the plane and put up a curtain around her for $7,000. Instead, I decided to call a friend of mine who owned a Lear jet. I tried every way to reach him; however, I learned that he and his family had gone to Hawaii and had not left any phone number where they could be reached.

I got on my knees, and I said, "Heavenly Father, I need that airplane. Please have him call me."

In less than five minutes, the hospital operator called me to the phone, and I heard the voice of my friend calling from Hawaii. He said, "Tom, five minutes ago I felt in my heart that the Lord was telling me to call you."

I said, "Five minutes ago I asked the Lord to have you call." It is wonderful to have a God Whom you can't ask for anything that He cannot do.

My friend asked me, "What can I do for you?"

I explained to him that I needed to move Pam from Alexandria, Virginia, to Denver, Colorado, by plane.

He said, "Thomas, tell me where and when you want the Lear, and it will be there." God used such dear friends as this all throughout Pam's illness to demonstrate the blessing of friendship and the power of God.

The pilot of the Lear jet stopped in Denver and picked up our family doctor, Ralph Roland, so he could monitor Pam during our flight from Virginia to Colorado. Dr. Roland admitted Pam to the St. Francis Hospital once we landed in Denver, and after two full weeks and many tests, the doctors in Denver confirmed that the East Coast doctors were correct: Pam's brain was dead.

A friend of mine had driven our motor home across the country, and it was now parked near the South Sheridan Baptist Church when I told Doctor Roland I wanted to bring Pam home. While Pam was in the hospital, she spiked very high fevers every other day. I told the doctors I believed it was due to my absence, because I was only able to see her every other day. I believed Pam in some way was aware of my presence and my absence, but some of the doctors only laughed at this explanation saying, "The fever was not connected to emotions." After two months in the hospital, we brought Pam home in May 1978; once we were home, the fevers ceased and never returned.

CHAPTER ELEVEN

❧

Years of Sustaining Faith

I WAS NOT TO KNOW THAT the storm would howl for a long twenty-eight and one-half years, but through each day God sustained me with what He taught me in the early days of faith. The doctor was correct when he warned me and said, "Tom, you don't know what you are getting into."

Bringing Pam home while still in a coma meant monitoring everything that went into her body, as well as everything that came out of her body. It meant figuring out what was causing her to hurt. It meant figuring out how to bathe her with tubes connected to her, while living inside a 40-foot motor home. Dividing my time and attention between Pam and the children was difficult as I wanted to be all I could be for each one. It became overwhelming to me to think that Pam could possibly wake up and see herself twisted and disfigured. She was so meticulous about her appearance before the meningitis attacked her body. Through this entire ordeal, God was my strength and help and gave me direction when I so desperately needed it.

He gave me the idea of how to bathe her using a 30-gallon trash barrel; I held Pam over the trash barrel while our two daughters, Phyllis and Penny, bathed their mother. Pam had long dark hair which was quite a lot of work to keep looking nice, and I was very proud of how the girls, who at this time were 17 and 11 years old, cared for her. I learned how to administer physical therapy on Pam when two physical therapists from St. Francis Hospital, Lil Ficket and Judy Graham, agreed to teach me. They came to our motor home and spent many hours helping me to learn the correct way to work with Pam so I would not damage the joints that needed to be straightened. One day when the ladies were teaching me physical therapy, Judy Graham said to me, "Mr. Williams, I have heard of the love of Jesus Christ, but now I have seen it in your love for your wife." That day Judy received Christ and was added to the family of God.

Amazingly enough, God was sustaining us financially with miracle after miracle. When Pam had been admitted to the hospital in Virginia and the business office discovered that we did not have insurance, the lady in charge called me to her office and said, "This bill will be thousands of dollars if your wife only lives a few days. How do you expect to pay such an exorbitant amount?"

I replied, "My Father will give me the money."

Incredulous, she asked, "Does your father have that much money?"

I confidently answered, "He sure does!"

"And he gives it to you?"

"Yes, Ma'am, He always has."

"Are you able to call him? We need three thousand dollars by 3:00 p.m. today."

"Yes, Ma'am. I know He's in because I was talking to Him when you called me to your office."

As I left the business office and stepped into the elevator to go to the ICU floor, I said, "Heavenly Father, this is Tom."

The Lord said, "I know it's you."

"Father, Pam is real sick."

"I know she is."

"Father, the hospital needs $3,000 today by 3:00 p.m."

It was wonderful to hear the Lord say, "Tom, I'll take care of it."

When I stepped off the elevator, I saw Dr. Bud Calvert, pastor of the Fairfax Baptist Temple in Fairfax, Virginia, walking down the hall toward me.

He asked, "Tom, where are you coming from?"

I answered, "I've been down at the business office. They told me they needed $3,000 today by 3:00 p.m."

He smiled and said, "Tom, our church prayed all night for you and Pam. As I was leaving the church early this morning, the men asked me to bring you a check for $3,500. We knew you would need some money, and they have agreed to put that much in the offering on Sunday."

Rejoicing in the Lord's provision and after thanking Pastor Calvert, I stepped back into the elevator and returned to the business office. I handed the check to the lady I had previously spoken to, and as she looked at the amount, she said, "This is remarkable."

Two days later the same lady called me into her office to inform me that the hospital needed $4,000 by 4:00 p.m.

"I'll call my Father about it," I told her.

Once again I stepped onto the elevator and told my Heavenly Father about the situation, and He assured me He would take care of it. I stepped off the elevator with peace in my heart. As I was walking past the nurses' station, the phone began to ring. No one was at the station at the time and since most calls had recently been for our family, I walked over and answered it. It was our pastor from Denver, Dr. Ed Nelson, calling to inquire after Pam's condition as well as about our financial needs. I told him the business office was requiring a $4,000 payment by 4:00 p.m. He said, "Praise the Lord, Tom! We took an offering for you last night, and the amount was $4,120. Ask Pastor Calvert to write you a check for $4,000 and tell him we will send him this money via express mail."

The day we were flying Pam from Virginia to Colorado, I had to

PRAYER AND FAITH:
The Life of Dr. Tom Williams

go to the business office to get Pam's release papers, and the same lady was there. She said, "Mr. Williams, I have worked in this hospital for 14 years, and we have never seen anything like this. So much money has come in for your bill that we owe you a refund, but it will take us about a week to get it to you."

I almost said, "Ma'am, I need it today by 4:00 p.m!" When I asked her about the bill for the internal specialist, Dr. Shih, she told me he had not submitted his bill and that I would need to talk with him. I spoke to him about it as he and I were walking down the hall behind the stretcher that was taking Pam to the ambulance. He said, "Mr. Williams, the reason there is no bill is, there is no bill." He had worked with Pam for six weeks, and God had touched his heart to forgive the entire bill.

We had been in Colorado for two months when I knew in my heart that God was directing me to go back on the road and just to trust Him. Needless to say, I was frightened as the doctors had told me Pam could go into a seizure or a convulsion at any time, and I had no idea what I would do if we were some place that was many miles from a hospital. God had shown Himself to be so capable and mighty in our earlier years that I was able to draw from those experiences and believe God to make the difference in this time of our ministry. As we began to travel again in the motor home, I continued to care for Pam and perform the therapy her body needed. I performed physical therapy on her all through the day and preached at night while the children stayed with their mother.

It was while we were in Knoxville, Tennessee, parked at a church where I was holding revival meetings, that God answered the children's prayer and brought Pam out of the coma. The children had been praying that the Lord would wake their mother up on my birthday, which was August 17; however, the Lord chose to wake her up on August 18. For months our youngest son Paul had brought a little stuffed dog we named Rainbow, because of its many colors, back to show his mother each night. Paul would hold Rainbow up in front of his mother's eyes and ask her, "Mother, who is this?"

Each night Pam just stared at the little dog and gave no reply; however, on August 18 Pam spoke and said as best she could, "Rainbow." The motor home became a hub of excitement and jubilation as we hugged one another and rejoiced in hearing Pam's voice after being silenced for six months. I dropped to my knees in front of her and said, "It's Tom, Honey! It's Tom," and she replied, "Tom."

I quickly called Dr. Roland in Colorado, and his response was, "Tom, I was hoping I would never have to tell you this, but what you have on your hands is a brand-new baby. Pam is just echoing everything she hears; she is not aware of what she is saying."

We praised the Lord she was no longer in the coma, but we soon realized what the doctor had said was true; Pam did not know anything, but she was very capable of echoing everything she heard. She did not know me or the children, and she was, in many ways, like a newborn baby needing to learn everything all over again.

Two months after Pam woke from the coma, she went into a seizure one day while we were in Puyallup, Washington, though I did not know at the time what was happening to her. I had not witnessed Pam's seizures in the hospital and had never seen anyone else have a seizure, so I was completely unprepared. We had been to lunch and were driving back to the motor home with our friends, Don Linkem and Jim Berry, when Pam went into the seizure.

I immediately cried out to God, "Oh Father, help!" as Don spun the car around and sped toward the hospital. He drove to the main entrance, and I picked Pam up in my arms and ran inside. A nurse led me to the emergency room and directed me to lay Pam on a bed while a doctor was summoned. The doctor rushed into the room to begin working on Pam, and once he had assessed the situation, he calmly said, "It's going to be okay, Mr. Williams; your wife is having a grand mal seizure, and she should come out of it soon." I'll never forget what my two friends said to me that day as we left the hospital, "That's the difference between our walks with God, isn't it? The first thing you thought of was God, and the first thing we thought of was the hospital. Real close communion with God draws you to Him in a crisis rather than to men." Pam's seizure that day was the first of many more she experienced through the years of her illness, but each time God carried us through with grace and help.

The next five years I spent countless hours retraining Pam, taking her through each stage a newborn baby goes through. The doctors told me that Pam would require a catheter for the rest of her life as she would not be able to control her bladder. I was told Pam would never be able to feed herself and she would never be able to walk again. I was told she would never again be able to do anything for herself. But God blessed the thousands of hours of therapy, and love paid off as Pam was finally able to do all of the things that we were told she would never do again.

Pam did learn to walk again, though she had a shuffling gait and needed my arm for steadying support on most occasions. Pam could feed herself, though I did have to cut and prepare her food. Pam was able to control her bladder, but she still needed assistance. Pam learned to do many things for herself, like putting on lipstick, tying her shoes, and other daily routines we take for granted. The Lord was so good in blessing like He did; however, He chose not to allow her to regain her mental abilities. Pam's mental abilities remained like that of a small child.

In the midst of her initial recovery, criticism came from numerous people who thought I was amiss in performing the therapy myself and that I should have professional therapists attending my wife. I contacted the Craig Rehabilitation Center in Colorado, which is world-renowned for their success. After four months of seeking an appointment with the top neurologist, one was granted. The physician asked me to bring Pam in and demonstrate all that she could do. When we arrived at the Rehab clinic, we were escorted to a room where a number of therapists from every field of therapy waited. Pam and I were given chairs in the center of the room where she was able to demonstrate all that she had learned from my hours of working with her. This neurologist had access to all of Pam's previous medical records and was aware that she had been declared brain-dead and that her prognosis for learning was completely hopeless.

When the demonstration was completed, the neurologist asked the therapists in the room, "Can any of you improve on what has been done?" Each therapist with tears in his eyes replied, "You know, doctor, that what we do, we do professionally, and professionalism cannot possibly do what love has done for this lady." The doctor then asked his secretary to bring a particular article from his office. He handed the article to me and asked me to read it.

The article told about a young man who was involved in a car wreck in Alaska, and this young man had lapsed into a coma as a result of his injuries from the wreck. He had been sent to the Craig Rehabilitation Center for help. The article stated that after 11 months of therapy, he could only slightly move, on command, his right index finger. He could not speak or make any other movements. His dad and mom made the decision to just take him home and make him as comfortable as possible with them.

This young man's brother met them at the airport in Alaska, which was the first time his brother had seen him since he went into a coma. His brother knelt down beside the stretcher, put his arms around him, and with tears dropping upon his face, called him by name and said, "I love you."

PRAYER AND FAITH:
The Life of Dr. Tom Williams

The young man on the stretcher reached up, put his arms around his brother, and said, "I love you too." As I finished reading the article, the doctor looked at me and said, "Mr. Williams, in five seconds love did what eleven months of the finest therapy in the world could not do." He further added, "Now, continue to take care of your wife and forget your critics."

As the trial continued, so did God's grace. I remember at one point when I was cast down as the Apostle Paul said of himself in the Scriptures that God poured out another sustaining balm to my weary heart. The children were marrying and leaving home one by one, the finances were a constant struggle, and the continued trial with Pam's illness brought such loneliness. I was in the kitchen crying out to the Lord for an encouragement that only He could give when the phone began to ring. I answered, and the secretary to Dr. Jack Hyles of First Baptist Church of Hammond, Indiana, was calling. She said, "Dr. Williams, Dr. Hyles would like for you to come to the Pastors' School and tell your story this coming March 1983." I was elated and thrilled as I knew that I would be speaking before thousands of pastors and their people. To me, that meant there would be an unbelievable amount of prayer to the Lord for our situation.

That night at Pastors' School, a number of others had given before me, their stories which were so moving and which also testified of the greatness of our God. The hour was late when it came my turn to get up and give the story, so I turned to Dr. Hyles and asked him how long he wanted me to take. His answer to me was, "Till you are through." The emotions in the building were already spent and were running high from all that God had done previously in others' lives, but I felt liberty from the Lord to give the entire story.

During the telling of the story, there were five standing ovations received to give honor to the mighty power of God. As I finished the story and asked our oldest son Tim to bring his mother to the platform, the response from the now-standing audience was absolutely deafening. From Dr. Hyles on the platform to the man sitting in the farthest balcony, I don't believe there were many dry eyes in that entire crowd.

My heart cried out, "Oh, Lord, my God, how great Thou art!"

After some moments, Dr. Hyles asked the crowd to be seated, and he said, "I would like for us to raise a $10,000 offering to help Brother Williams with the expenses for the caretaker he has to help with his wife." The service closed that night, and Dr. Hyles asked me if it would be possible for Pam and me to be in the 9:00 a.m. service the next morning. That next morning Dr. Hyles presented Mrs. Williams with a platform rocker that might in some way help her to be more comfortable each day. He then asked me to step to the podium and said to me, "We wanted to raise a $10,000 offering for you, but we received a little more than that." He smiled and said, "I'm sure that you can use it." He then said, "Let me present you with the largest love offering that Pastors' School has ever given anyone." He presented me with a check that exceeded $38,000. Following Pastors' School, invitations began to come in from around the world to come and present the story to churches and colleges.

We were invited again in 1984 to give the story at Pastors' School. Sometime during the year between the two Pastors' Schools, I had spoken privately to Dr. Hyles about making a film of the story. Following the presentation of the story in 1984, a spontaneous offering was taken to help make the film a reality. Dr. Hyles presented the offering to me the next morning in a humorous way as he said, "Brother Williams, here is a check for $25,000 for the making of the film." I thanked him and the people, then turned to walk away when he said, "Oh, I forgot something," and handed me another check for $25,000!

By the time that we had the story written as a script for a film, interviewed actors for the film, and filmed all of nine minutes, the money had been spent. I prayed for one entire year, but the money only trickled in. Many were saying to me that evidently the Lord did not want a film made.

In my heart I knew that God wanted the film to be made and shown around the world. I went to a small church in the northeast part of our nation to preach, and on Sunday morning a gentleman whom I had never met said, "Are you Dr. Tom Williams?" I told him that I was Dr. Tom Williams, and then he asked me about the progress of the film.

I said, "We have not been able to continue making the film because of finances."

He said, "I would like to give you a check this morning for $100,000." The making of the film never stopped again as God wonderfully sent in the remaining money that was needed. An 80-minute, first-class motion picture filmed in Israel and America was previewed at the First Baptist Church of Hammond on a Sunday night in December of 1985. Dr. Hyles and the people there were overwhelmed at the quality and the message of the film, "Twice Given." It has since been shown in more than 130 nations around the world. Millions of people have been blessed and challenged for Christ while countless others have come to know Jesus Christ as their personal Saviour.

As a result of God's favor shown to us through Pastors' School and the making of the film, I began receiving more meetings than ever before. Being directed by God, I moved my family to Murfreesboro, Tennessee, so I could be centrally located among the populace of our country, since 80 percent of America lives east of the Mississippi River. Our move to Murfreesboro was not without its trials, and once again I was asked by the Lord to exercise faith in Him. Having the experiences from the early years of our ministry, I was able to draw strength and assurance that God would meet our needs as wonderfully as He had always done in the past.

Three days before we were to leave Colorado and begin our move to Tennessee, the bank in Tennessee called and said, "We have decided you are too big a risk and are declining your loan." I gave myself to prayer and called upon the Lord for direction. He directed me to call a businessman in Florida who had always told me to call him if there was ever anything he could do for the ministry. I called this man, told him my situation with the bank in Tennessee, and this man asked me for the bank's name and the name of the president of that bank. He then called the bank's president, stating that he would sign a guarantee that he would pay for anything if I was unable to make payments.

Due to the tremendous business and financial status of this man, the bank agreed to grant me the loan. The situation actually turned out quite humorous as the president of the bank asked me, "Mr. Williams, is there anything else you would like to buy?" when he called to tell me the bank would grant me the loan.

My faith was to be tested further on the day of our move. The moving van came and loaded everything, and while the truck was being loaded, my youngest daughter needed to take care of last-minute school obligations across town. The moving van was loaded and had just left when I received a phone call from my daughter saying she had wrecked the car. I praise God she wasn't hurt, but it vastly changed our travel arrangements. My wife, my daughter, and Becky, the young lady helping to take care of Pam at that time, were to drive the car to Tennessee while I followed them in our pickup pulling a horse trailer.

Our pickup was bulging with boxes, but with a little rearranging, we were all four able to fit. Traveling to Tennessee this way made it a very difficult trip for all of us and especially for Pam. However, once

PRAYER AND FAITH:

The Life of Dr. Tom Williams

again God comforted my heart with a peace that passed understanding and gave me full assurance that though there are trials, I was in the very center of His will in moving my family to Tennessee.

It was wonderful now to be flying out of Nashville, which was the hub for two major airlines, and we could reach our destination without the inconvenience of changing planes. I was taking Pam with me on the planes, and though she could walk for the first few years of her illness, it was still difficult getting her on and off the planes.

We made Murfreesboro our home base for the next five years as we traveled and served the Lord. In 1988, through unusual circumstances, the Lord led me to move the ministry to Missouri and begin running a beautiful 2,800-acre ranch nestled in the foothills of the Ozark Mountains. The children were now all married and living in homes of their own, but Pam, her caregiver Pam, my sister and brother-in-law, Herb and Juanita Grover, and my secretary, Sue Steele, along with her two daughters, Wendy and Kristy, moved with us to Missouri.

The ranch was a dream come true, but to manage this dream required a large staff. I needed to have extra help working in the pastures, cleaning the guest cabins, preparing meals in the restaurant kitchen, and extra help in the office. I was able to hire four families and several single people to fill these positions. The Lord blessed the move from Tennessee and blessed the assembling of the staff, and Circle B Ranch was born.

The accessories that came with the ranch were unbelievable. We were able to offer our guests stagecoach rides, covered wagon rides, a miniature golf course, an old-fashioned carousel, a train for children to ride, several athletic fields, a swimming pool, an exercise room with all the latest equipment, 32 small lakes for fishing, horseback riding, and abundant wildlife. The ranch was a dream for this cowboy as it also came equipped with 55 head of horses and an indoor riding arena. Honeymoon couples, families, widow ladies, singles, and couples needing marital counseling began to come from all over America.

My faith now was being stretched to greater heights as the monthly budget for the ranch was $60,000. I was constantly traveling to promote the ranch, and while at the ranch, I was working about 18 hours a day. The staff we had was wonderful, and many even wore multiple hats, but it still wasn't enough for this size of a ranch. God was sending in miraculous amounts of money, yet the monthly budget just wasn't being met. I knew I couldn't continue at this pace and adequately be what Pam needed.

In the autumn of 1990, I let all the staff go, except for the two ladies Sherry and Pam that helped to care for Pam, and we moved off the ranch.

So many people have asked me through the years, "Was Circle B Ranch a mistake?"

I can say today what I said then, "It was not a mistake to know that couples were helped, to know that many were kept from the divorce courts, to know that families were blessed and experienced one of the greatest vacations of their lives, to hear widow ladies say they felt safe and secure while on the ranch, to know that many souls were brought to Christ, and to have had such an impact on newlyweds beginning their lives together." God makes no mistakes but takes us from faith to faith.

CHAPTER TWELVE

Abundant Grace

IN I TIMOTHY 1:14 PAUL TELLS US about grace that is exceeding abundant. This is the only kind of grace that had and would help me with all of the ups and downs of Pam's condition. I recall the abundant grace God gave me from the time she was in the coma to the apex of her condition. Grace did not flow like a river; it simply came like the stream in the desert to the thirsty soul, which was enough for each day.

I remember the morning I woke up and went to help Pam out of bed, but she could not walk. The doctors told me this would happen one day and that it would be sudden; however, that knowledge did not remove the dread that welled up in my heart that morning. The thousands of hours that I had spent teaching her to walk was now forever gone. This time there would be no retraining; it was just a fact that she would never walk again. With no choice remaining, I had to put Pam in a wheelchair.

For years I had battled the thought of her being in a wheelchair because, to me, it was as if I had given up on her ever walking normally again. I cried till I was spent, prayed, and beseeched the Lord to allow her to continue to walk, and throughout the day I tried to help Pam to walk. Though I was confused and heartbroken, God's grace flooded my soul with peace that this was now His will for us. From that day on, the wheelchair became an integral part of our lives; it went everywhere that we did.

Another nightmare that I battled was a wheelchair lift for our vehicle. To me, installing one was admitting that Pam would not walk again and forever be wheelchair bound, so I continued to lift Pam in and out of the car for a number of years. In a hotel in Michigan one day, I was on my knees battling with the Lord concerning what I was to do about a wheelchair lift when the gates of my soul suddenly opened, pouring forth a flood of grace and causing me to cry, "My Father, I want Your will!"

As tears continued to roll down my face, I went to Pam and her caregiver at that time, Jeannine Baldwin, and said, "The Lord won the battle; we are getting a van with a chairlift." The miracle that so encouraged us was that by the end of the day, a gentleman had bought us a van with a chairlift.

Pam had not experienced any grand mal seizures for a period of about four years, but one day in 1996 I noticed Pam's face lock and her eyes roll back in her head as her body began to convulse. I ran to her, and as swiftly and gently as I could, I laid her on the floor with her head in my lap as my heart cried out to God, "Oh, Lord, help her!" The flood of emotions that filled my heart that day was overwhelming; my heart broke for her as I had to witness again the horribleness of what the seizures did to her. My heart also ached at what was ahead because the seizures came so suddenly and without warning.

I cried, "Lord, not again, for her sake and for ours." I felt my emotions had reached the end of their ability to cope with the years of loneliness, fright, adjustments, and always the thought of death. These emotions held the fear of her having a seizure, of not being able to help her come out of the seizure, and of the seizure's taking her life. The great amount of responsibility was heavier than I felt I could bear, but once more God's exceeding, abundant grace carried me through when it seemed I would fall under the load. On days such as this, I was so thankful God's grace was never withheld.

CHAPTER TWELVE
Abundant Grace

I continued to persevere for the sake of my sweetheart, yet in late 1997 she went from experiencing grand mal seizures to what we were told was called status epilepticus (prolonged or serial seizures). This new type of seizure meant she would not come out of the seizure without prescription medicine administered directly into her blood stream. This progression in her disease catapulted us into a completely new realm; we now had to carry syringes and vials of prescription medicine everywhere we went.

It was never easy to watch the doctors or nurses give Pam shots, and the difficulty quadrupled now that I was the one to administer the injection of the medicine. Questions flooded my mind.

- "Would I do it right?"
- "Would I get it in a muscle which would cause great pain to her?"
- "Would the first shot work, or would another one have to be given in another few moments?"

These thoughts and others like them ran through my mind each time that Pam now went into a seizure. What drove me on was the thought that I was doing all I could to help the one I loved. "He giveth more grace when the burdens grow greater" are beautiful words in a song, yet they are also words that describe a tremendous truth because without God's grace I never could have continued on.

With every seizure, Pam lost a little bit more of her physical abilities, and traveling became difficult for all of us. Gradually I began to leave Pam and her caregiver at home and traveled alone. In early 1999 Pam had a seizure which almost took her life. Then I decided I was only going to preach at weekend meetings so I could be home with Pam throughout the week. Because I was traveling less, I had to make a decision concerning the ministry. God had given us a beautiful home on 28 acres, which also included a bunk house, a barn, a warehouse, a 5,000-square foot office building, and a 3-bedroom home. The bunk house and 3-bedroom home housed the two families He brought to work for our ministry. I had to make the decision to sell our headquarters for the ministry and let my employees go and relocate.

I had tried to move to Georgia a couple of years earlier to be closer to our oldest daughter Phyllis and her family; however, the Lord never opened the door for that opportunity to happen. As I began to pray and ask the Lord to direct me where to move, I once again prayed about moving to Georgia as well as maybe just moving to a different location in Murfreesboro, but God did not open either one of these doors. After these doors closed, I believed the Lord was leading me to purchase a place out West.

I first pursued something in South Dakota; however, God closed that door as well. During a conversation with my youngest daughter concerning our move, she said, "Dad, if you're going to move out West, why don't you consider moving to Montana close by Don and me?" I knew Penny had been through so much because of her mother's illness, and I thought her suggestion would be an answer to some healing for both of our hearts.

In August we flew out to look at some properties Penny had found. As we walked through the place at 7285 Thorpe Road in Belgrade, Montana, God spoke to my heart and said, "Tom, this is home." Within one month's time, God had sold our place in Murfreesboro, and we, with the help of many friends, moved out to Montana.

The next step in Pam's decline came when she could no longer maintain her balance while sitting in a chair. Many times we had to prop her up on one side with pillows to keep her from falling. When it became evident it was no longer safe for her anymore, we had to put her in a hospital bed with siderails. Seeing her in that hospital bed caused my heart to sink even more because it had such a finality to it. I had always tried to keep some small spark of hope alive that she would one day improve again, but this was as if a huge door had been slammed shut and locked.

The portion of grace that God poured out at that time was once again sufficient to meet the battle and to go on. Again I fought a battle inside of myself and would not use the Hoyer lift because I wanted to keep the spark of hope alive that she wouldn't get worse, that God would hear my pleas to restore her.

The tremendous responsibility and greater physical labor required in caring for Pam became too great for one person alone. Though God had provided Pat Phares, Malisa Dingman, and Vera Culp at different times for extra help in caring for Pam, the bulk of responsibility lay on Jeannine when I was gone during the weekends. She experienced many of Pam's seizures while alone with her. The strain, both physically and emotionally, began to take a toll on her health as she had now been with Pam for nine years. This and the fact that now two people were required to properly care for Pam, I cancelled all of my meetings and discontinued traveling.

God had called me to preach, and as any man called to preach would know, when a man is called to preach, there is "preach" in him that must come out. I began to wonder how I could stay at home and not preach. Other thoughts permeated my mind such as, "If I don't travel and preach, will our prayer support decrease? I won't be in front of the people, telling them of our story nor of Pam's condition. Will the people forget about praying for us?"

So many people told me that we would starve if I didn't travel and preach because the love offerings at these meetings were our main source of income. However, I knew deep in my heart that God would provide, and I answered, "But I still have God."

The thought that troubled me was the uncertainty of how long I would have to remain home without going out and preaching. The

PRAYER AND FAITH:

The Life of Dr. Tom Williams

gift of grace God gave me then and had been teaching me for so many years was that I had to continue to live this journey day by day. God is serious when He says, *"Take therefore no thought for the morrow: for the morrow shall take thought for the things of itself. Sufficient unto the day is the evil thereof."* (Matthew 6:34) My blessed Lord also challenged me with the *"fowls of the air"* and *"the lilies of the field"* because they do nothing, yet God provides for them.

The blessed Holy Spirit reminded me of what He had told me after our terrible car wreck in 1965, which left me, for a time, unable to provide for my family. His ability to provide was not dependent on my ability to travel. God allowed me to swim in an ocean of His grace by keeping the door open for me to preach on the radio. That program is now being heard all over the world because of Internet access. He also granted me the desire of my heart, which, for years, had been to persuade men to pray, but now the Lord was saying to me, "Tom, don't just preach on prayer; start a school of prayer."

In 2002 God began sending pastors, missionaries, widows, businessmen, and entire families who had a desire to learn how to pray to Montana, and our school of prayer was born. The blessings of the school of prayer began to spread across the nation as people returned home, changed in their prayer life. Our motto, "Not a prayer *time*, but a prayer *life*," began to be echoed all over the country. God took the school of prayer and extended it to Pastors' School as Dr. Jack Schaap invited me to come teach it there.

Dr. Schaap has continued to love and help our ministry just as his father-in-law, Dr. Jack Hyles, did by taking special offerings and inviting me to preach in the church and college. God has also extended it to the mission field via a cell phone ministry. He extended it to national prayer crusades, and He extended it to teaching it as a 15-hour course at Bible colleges. When situations look bleak, God takes them and causes our hearts to sing, "All hail the power of

Jesus' name, let angels prostrate fall, bring forth the royal diadem and crown Him Lord of all!"

It has always been a blessing to me to know that God never throws us into the trial head-first, but He walks us in gradually—one step at a time. The hospital bed was a great trial to face, as I said, but it seemed easier to face now that Pam was aspirating and having great difficulty swallowing. Pam's dysphagia added a new element of concern as we cared for her, but God had seen the complete outlaying of our lives and had made preparation for the needed hour.

Jeannine had been a speech pathologist and had been trained in the symptoms, signs, causes, and treatments of dysphagia before coming to care for Pam many years earlier. Her specialized training was a tremendous help in correctly diagnosing and determining the safest way to feed Pam. As Pam's swallowing deficiency grew more severe, I began to fear what would occur because many doctors were advising me not to consider a feeding tube again. They felt I should just let Pam go.

The uncertainty of whether or not I would have to make a decision for a feeding tube was a constant weight on my heart because I certainly could not let Pam starve to death. I began to pray, "Heavenly Father, would You add Your mercy to Your grace and let Pam slip Home to Heaven in her sleep?" He graciously answered that prayer on October 5, 2006. At 1:00 a.m. I checked on Pam. Jeannine or I checked on Pam many times at night to be sure she was in the correct sleeping position to prevent her from aspirating on her own saliva. At 1 a.m. when I checked on Pam, she was sleeping peacefully. When I checked on her again at 4:00 a.m., Pam had graduated and found rest in the presence of her Lord.

CHAPTER THIRTEEN

Channels of Blessing

THROUGH THE TRIAL OF PAM'S illness, there came a number of what I guess you would call side effects that God brought into people's lives because of our trial. God's picture is so much greater than what we see; it is like an embroidered piece of cloth. On one side is a beautiful finished product, whereas on the other side is a garbled weaving of thread in which a pattern is barely discernible. Or it can be equated to a sculptor who looks at a piece of rock and sees an image that only his eye can discern, the way Mr. Borglum saw four Presidents' faces when everyone else just saw a mountain of granite. Many times God uses us as channels of blessings as He weaves His workings in others' lives.

I remember preaching in Marathon, New York, telling the story of Pam's illness and describing the great strength we had received thus far from God, enabling us to continue serving Him. The church was packed to capacity, and I had come to a point in telling the story which was capturing the attention of the audience down to the smallest child.

A lady suddenly stood to her feet and cried, "My God, my God, this man can love this woman through this type of trial..." and turning to the man sitting beside her said, "...while you and I are living in adultery! We will be married immediately, or you are moving out. I cannot imagine continuing living like we are when there is a love which we could know similar to this." The pastor told me that this couple did get married and became steadfast Christians for the Lord.

⚮

I was preaching on the radio in Kansas City, Missouri, and had been asked by the owner of the station to tell the radio listeners about our trial and how the depths of our faith had been tried. Just as I had finished speaking and gone off the air, the telephone in the studio rang. The receptionist told us it was a man calling to speak to me. I accepted the call, and the caller said, "I just finished listening to your story, and I need your prayers. My wife and I are divorced. God broke my heart as I listened to your story, and I thought our reasons for divorcing seemed so petty compared to your situation. Would you pray for us as I am going to drive right now across the city and talk to my ex-wife. I want to tell her what I just heard and somehow relay to her how broken my heart is over our divorce. Please pray that God will put us back together again and help me to love her as you love your wife."

Little did he or I know that his wife had been listening to the same program and was driving to find him because God also had smitten her heart about their divorce. Though they missed one another, they continued searching, and later that evening finally found each other. He called me the next morning to tell me what had transpired and to tell me that God had rejoined their hearts to unite once more in marriage and this time to put Him first. Three days later the pastor there was privileged to perform the ceremony, and praise be to God, a home was saved!

⚮

While I was in Dallas, Texas, holding revival meetings, I told our story on a Sunday evening. Later that night a young couple, while in their home, saw their little baby girl begin to grow very sick, so they rushed her to the hospital. The doctor's examination of the baby revealed that she had meningitis, and her condition was growing worse by the hour. The doctors met with the couple a short while later to tell them their baby would probably not live till morning.

The young couple looked at the doctor and decidedly said, "Doctor, we will be in the hospital chapel on our knees. You come and tell us when the baby is well." They prayed throughout the night, and early the next morning the doctor found them to say, "I do not understand, but you may take your baby home. She is completely well."

Monday night in the meeting, they were testifying and praising God for His mercy. They said, "Brother Williams, we would never have had the faith to believe God would heal her had we not heard your story yesterday." I think of the song "Channels Only," and if we would keep the truths of this song in mind, it would make our trials much easier to bear.

I received a phone call from a man in Florida who had been given a copy of my itinerary, and he asked, "Brother Williams, you are going to be preaching about two hours from where I live. Would it be possible to meet with you so I could tell you my story? I could drive over and take you out for a meal if that would work into your schedule." Agreeing to his request, I met him at a restaurant the next day. To my surprise, the man was a physical giant. I'm six feet tall and weigh 210 pounds; yet this man put a hand on each side of my arms and picked me up off the ground to hug me and put a kiss on my cheek. Tears were streaming down his face like a brokenhearted child. He said, "You have no idea how much I love you in the Lord though we have never met."

As we sat down to eat, he began to tell me his story, "My wife and I had a three-year-old boy. He was the sunrise, the sunset, and everything in-between to us. I don't know if you can understand how devastated I was when the doctors told us he had cancer. I thought

PRAYER AND FAITH:
The Life of Dr. Tom Williams

I would lose my mind, and then one day someone brought me a tape of your testimony. I listened to your story every day for one entire year. God used your testimony to help me watch my little boy gradually slip away to Heaven. I just had to see you and tell you what you mean to me."

Dr. Jack Hyles asked me one time, "How do you keep going?"

I said, "It sure does help to know God uses the story."

❧

I was preaching in another part of Florida at a different time when a man and his wife asked to speak to me after the service. They told me she had a very rare disease; she could not eat or drink anything by mouth. She was fed by a machine that was attached to her chest. The couple explained to me that only 20 people in the entire world had this disease. To operate this machine was extremely expensive and had literally bankrupted them. Their insurance would not continue to pay, so they sold their home, and all of that money had been used toward this machine.

Someone had taken them the book I had written, entitled *Loving My Wife Back to Health*. The story gave them the faith to believe God and to get down on their knees asking Him to care for their needs. The same week they had read the book, a man whom they did not know called and told them he had been reading about her disease and the cost of it in a medical journal. He also told them he was going to pay for all of their expenses for as long as she lived.

I thought of the message that was first sent across the transatlantic telegraph cable, "What hath God wrought!"

❧

Sitting in one section of the Gospel Light Baptist Church in Walkertown, North Carolina, where I was holding meetings, were 13 couples. In the lap of each lady sat a Down syndrome child, and though this was a large church, that was still an unusual sight to see.

After the service, these 13 couples approached me asking if they could possibly meet with me.

Once I finished with other responsibilities, which was about 9:30 p.m., we all sat down together. The couples explained they were part of a club they had formed to encourage each other in their situation. They said, "Though this club has been a tremendous help to us and we have been able to encourage one another, there remains one question that we all need answered. How do we face a lifetime of heartache? These children will never graduate from high school let alone go to college; they will never marry or experience any of the milestones in one's usual lifetime. We know your wife has been sick now for a number of years, and from a realistic perspective, she is never going to be well. How do you remain objective and continue to serve the Lord and be used by Him?"

I answered, "First of all, you only live one day at a time, and as in everything else, the Word of God is our strength. In Jeremiah 29:11 it says, *'For I know the thoughts that I think toward you, saith the LORD, thoughts of peace, and not of evil, to give you an expected end.'* If you can keep in mind that God will use this in your life to help someone else, that thought will sustain you as you go through the trial. II Corinthians 1:3, 4 says, *'Blessed be God, even the Father of our Lord Jesus Christ, the Father of mercies, and the God of all comfort; Who comforteth us in all our tribulation, that we may be able to comfort them which are in any trouble, by the comfort wherewith we ourselves are comforted of God.'*" I then asked each couple to share the burdens that lay on their hearts, and with a great emotional release they did so until 1:30 in the morning. When they were finished, we formed a circle and held hands while I committed all of us into the tender loving care of our Heavenly Father, closing by asking Him to help us all be a testimony of His goodness.

PRAYER AND FAITH:
The Life of Dr. Tom Williams

During a revival meeting in Alabama, I was introduced one night to six ladies who had driven from Georgia to be there, hoping I would be able to spend some time with them after the service to help them with their trials. Following the service, we were given a room to meet in. One by one each lady described her situation. The first lady who spoke said, "As you can see, my face is disfigured because I was in a horrible car wreck. My husband left me because I am no longer beautiful."

The second lady said, "My mom and dad were both killed in a car wreck one week ago."

The third lady told me she was dying of cancer, and she didn't know how to tell her children goodbye.

The fourth lady said, "I have lost both of my breasts, and now I feel completely unattractive to my husband."

The fifth lady said, "My husband has been unfaithful, and I don't know how to continue to love him."

The last lady told me she had just buried two children less than one month apart. They felt that since I had buried a wife, a baby, and now had a mentally and physically impaired wife, I could be of help to them with what God had taught me. I spent nearly five hours with them, listening to their stories and counseling them from the Scriptures and from my experiences. I said to the first lady, " '... *for the* LORD *seeth not as man seeth; for man looketh on the outward appearance, but the* LORD *looketh on the heart,*' (I Samuel 16:7) In God's sight, you are beautiful. Your husband has forsaken you because his love was not genuine, but your God will never forsake you because His love is pure. You must do what I have done; find your joy and your peace in the Lord."

To the second lady I said, "It is never easy when a loved one is taken, but especially when it is very sudden, and to have both parents taken the same day is an emotional roller coaster. David said in

Psalm 23:1, 2, '*The* LORD *is my shepherd; I shall not want. He maketh me to lie down in green pastures: he leadeth me beside the still waters.*' This is a time when we have to believe in the sovereignty of God and know that He makes no mistakes."

I said to the third lady, "This is a path I have not walked. I've never had to tell my children I was dying, but I have had to tell my two wives and my baby goodbye. My suggestion to you would be to fix a meal for your entire family, invite your pastor and his wife to come, and then following the meal have the children sit next to you and your husband. As they gather next to you, explain to them the severity of your illness saying something like, 'As we have invited pastor and his wife for supper, God has invited me to soon come to Heaven, but I want you to remember this supper time and know that we will be together again at supper time in Heaven.'"

I said to the fourth lady, "Do not judge your husband's love by what he is doing or not doing in the midst of this trial. You must remember that as you have not been through this trial before, neither has he. Satan will lie to you about your husband's feelings and physical attraction for you and seek to draw you into a pity party. Your husband probably feels as awkward as you do about what has happened to your body. I encourage you just to love him and act like, as much as possible, nothing has happened."

I told the fifth lady, "I have counseled many couples in similar situations and have told them, as I am going to tell you, there will never be any repair to the marriage or sincere regained trust unless there is full forgiveness. There is no way to justify what he has done, but I would suggest that you thoroughly examine your life to see if there wasn't more that could have been done to prevent it. If you discover something in your life where you were not as good a wife as you could have been in every way, then go to him and ask him to forgive you for not being all you could have been. I promise you, seeking his forgiveness will go a long way in bringing him to a real repentance concerning what he has done to you."

To the last lady I said, "I buried my wife and my daughter four months and four days apart. That much sorrow, just like the second lady's sorrow, is hard to process." I told her not to hold back her emotions, but that God had given us tears as vents to our soul. Additionally, I said to her, "The Scripture tells us in Ecclesiastes 3:4, there is 'A *time to weep,...a time to mourn....*' The Lord knew these times would come and arranged for grace to help us in such a great time of need. Remember Jesus said in Matthew 11:28-30, '*Come unto me, all ye that labour and are heavy laden, and I will give you rest. Take my yoke upon you, and learn of me; for I am meek and lowly in heart: and ye shall find rest unto your souls. For my yoke is easy, and my burden is light.*' Let me tell you last of all that Peter said in I Peter 5:7, '*Casting all your care upon him; for he careth for you.*'" At the close of our time together, we had a wonderful time of prayer as we each laid our tremendous burdens upon our everlasting Father.

Perhaps the greatest channel of blessings to others came when a young lady from Maryland sent Dr. James Dobson of *Focus on the Family* a cassette tape of our story that she had heard me give. After listening to the story, Dr. Dobson called me and asked me to come to their ministry headquarters to be interviewed. *Focus on the Family*, at that time, was located in California, and most of our upcoming meetings were being held on the East Coast. Dr. Dobson agreed to call me while I was in Maryland and interview me over the phone.

Following the interview, our story, called "Twice Given," was then aired on *Focus on the Family* radio network. We called the story "Twice Given" because my wife Pam was given to me following the death of my first wife and given back again from the throes of death.

Dr. Dobson estimated that twelve million people had listened to the radio broadcast because of the tremendous response they received by mail. The response to our story was the greatest response *Focus on the Family* had ever received. I have been told that for many years the only story that grew a greater response than ours was "Twice Pardoned." Dr. Dobson renamed our story "Loving My Wife Back to Health" when it was aired on their radio broadcast. *Focus on the Family* continued to run our story once or twice each year for many years to come.

Dr. Dobson also asked permission to have our audio interview dubbed into Spanish and sent it all over the Spanish-speaking world; then sometime later he dubbed it into the Russian language as well. I appreciate everything that Dr. Dobson and *Focus on the Family* have done over the years to make our story a channel of blessing to millions of others.

Our film was eventually dubbed into Spanish and Greek, and God blessed it as it went to the Spanish-speaking countries and to Greece. God also opened the door for the film to be shown on the Family channel as well as on Billy Graham's Association Network and in many churches and colleges. As a result, we received calls and letters from many parts of the world telling us how the film had been such a help and a blessing. What an encouragement it was to us for God to use our lives to touch so many others! It was a road we would not have chosen, and certainly a difficult one, but where it led, by the hand of God, was unbelievable.

CHAPTER FOURTEEN

The New Beginning

IN THE BIBLE WE SEE the wonderful truth of replacement. For instance, we see the Lord's giving Seth to Adam and Eve when Abel is taken. We notice that the Lord gave Hannah other children when she gave Samuel to Him. We read of the tremendous story of Job and how God gave him children again to replace the ones who had been slain. We also see the Lord's giving Abraham his wife, Keturah, after Sarah died.

Even as God provided a replacement for these, He also did the same for me by giving me Jeannine Baldwin, the young lady who cared for Pam for the last and most difficult 13 years of Pam's illness. Jeannine possessed so many of the godly characteristics a man desires for a wife as well as physical beauty. Through the years she had displayed courage, godliness, and an overwhelming desire to do the will of God. During the 13 years that she worked as Pam's care-giver, I met her family. I also learned of her tenaciousness; she labored steadily to receive her bachelor of arts and master of arts degrees in speech pathology. She carried out her childhood dream and rode her bicycle across America when the opportunity present-ed itself to her.

As a young teenager, Jeannine had read Peter Jenkins' book, *Walk Across America,* and was so impressed that she declared that some day she also would make such a venture. Jeannine was part of a humanity club on her college campus, and volunteers had been sought to ride bicycles across the country as a fund raiser to aid third-world countries. Jeannine's hand shot up as she exclaimed in her heart, "Here's my chance to go across America."

On June 16, 1986, in San Francisco, California, Jeannine joined other college students, young people, and adults of varying ages who made up this group who would ride 3,300 miles across the country to New York City, their final destination. Jeannine experienced heat fatigue riding across the salt flats of Utah, yet she kept riding. She experienced pulled back muscles; still she didn't want to give up her bicycle and rode through pain until her bicycle was taken from her by the others in her group who were seeking to protect her from further injury. She was back on the bicycle in two days. Throughout her ride, Jeannine demonstrated a tenacious drive to complete what she had set out to accomplish, which many of the riders in the group noticed and mentioned. Jeannine did not learn this trait suddenly on the ride; rather, she had steadily learned it from childhood to her teen years and on into adulthood.

During high school she played volleyball and basketball and learned to persevere and work hard when the talent wasn't always naturally supplied. Her volleyball coach told her later on, "I didn't cut you that first year because I saw potential and a young lady I could tell would work hard and take direction." She worked hard at improving her skills and became a frequent face in the local newspapers as throughout high school she became known as "the wall" in volleyball because of her consistent blocking success. This tenacity she exhibited carried over into her walk with the Lord, and God used it to encourage her not to quit when circumstances grew to levels of difficulty that were extraordinary.

There were many reasons why Jeannine went on to faithfully complete college and graduate school, but what I have gleaned from knowing her and her family was that she had an overwhelming desire to please her parents because higher education was their desire for their children. This quality was very evident in her walk with the Lord as she sought constantly to please Him, regardless of her own desires. Her testimony is that of being saved as an eight-year-old child, but never giving Him her life completely until she was 20 years old. She had wandered from God's path to walk down her own path for about four years until God gripped her heart and told her, "Jeannine, you gave Me your heart as a child, but you have never given Me your life. It's time to live for Me." She promised the Lord that day she would do all she could to possibly live for Him and do what He desired of her. Upon finishing graduate school, God asked her to move from her home state of California to begin working at a job on the East Coast in Norwalk, Connecticut. He was asking her to move away from family and all that was familiar to a place unknown and where there was neither family nor friends. Her desire had been to move back by her parents and siblings, but she desired more to please the Lord and had already learned a hard lesson in obedience the previous year.

Less than three short years later, God asked her to give up all she had studied and leave her speech pathology career to work for Him full-time by taking care of my wife Pam. We were holding a three-day meeting at Lighthouse Baptist Church in Norwalk, Connecticut, where Jeannine attended, when God spoke to her. She was in her backyard reading my book, *You Can Make It*, when God said, "Jeannine, you will be Pam's next nurse." She has testified that it was as if God bodily sat next to her and spoke, so she turned her head and answered, stopping herself mid-sentence as she realized there wasn't anyone there. She was willing to work for the Lord full-time, but her heart did not desire to move again into the unknown as He was once again asking her to leave all that was familiar—her church family and friends she had grown to love—to go to that which was unfamiliar once more where there weren't any family or friends.

She grappled with this decision for a few weeks until early one morning when she went to her special place by the bay and poured out her heart to the Lord as she walked up and down the pier. She pleaded with Him to let her stay in Connecticut, but He answered her with, "Read Act 8:26 and 27." After she read, "*And the angel of the Lord spake unto Philip, saying, Arise, and go toward the south unto the way that goeth down from Jerusalem unto Gaza, which is desert. And he arose and went: and, behold, a man of Ethiopia, an eunuch of great authority under Candace queen of the Ethiopians, who had the charge of all her treasure, and had come to Jerusalem for to worship,*" she knew she must comply and go.

All of these qualities she had would become necessary when she began caring for Pam as we flew 125,000 miles and drove another 25,000 miles the first year she was with us. Many of these trips began at five in the morning, and due to the schedule of meetings, there wasn't any time to rest until after the service at night. It wasn't long before I began to discover the spiritual side of this young lady; she constantly studied her Bible and read the Bible countless hours to Pam.

My prayer life includes a number of hours a day. As she joined in prayer, I heard her weep over the kids, by name, from her bus route that she had left in Connecticut. Along with this her prayers were fervent for unsaved college friends and for others who were struggling in their walk for the Lord. She often prayed for loved ones who needed to be saved and others who needed to be strengthened in their service for Christ.

I was so thrilled when I heard her from memory pray for the many widow ladies, pastors, cities, and countries for which she had heard me pray. She had learned to be burdened for them and to speak their names before the Lord. She was also a witness for Christ, and I remember one time at a rest stop when she and Pam had been so long in the ladies' room that I grew concerned. As I neared the door, I could hear her inside telling another lady how she could know the Saviour.

One of the most astounding things to me was that she gave up a lucrative job to come and work for us for considerably less. Though she was now making less, she was continuing to give as I suspect she had always given because her pastor in Connecticut told me she was the largest giver in their church. Her patience in caring for Pam was unbelievable; because of Pam's mental deficiencies, she would repeat the same phrases multiple times a day. When dealing with someone like Pam, the responses had to be given as though she had never spoken the phrase before. Jeannine was able to do this, largely in part due to her training, and she was also able to facilitate further conversation with Pam.

When Jeannine worked in the hospital as a speech pathologist, she did not have to change any of her patients' diapers. If that was necessary to do during a session, she always opted to call in the patient's attending nurse because she was adamant when she stated, "I did not go to school to be a registered nurse; I went to school to be a speech pathologist. There isn't any way I could ever change an adult's diaper." It became known all over the hospital that Jeannine was never going to change one of her patients' diapers, and her refusal became the joke of the rehab floor.

After one year with us, Pam was becoming incontinent, and it became necessary for Jeannine to change an adult's diaper. She rose to the occasion like a real trooper and never complained. I have often heard her say to others, "God has a wonderful sense of humor. Be careful what you say you will never do."

Over the years Jeannine also showed her abilities in cooking and performing other household duties as she assumed many other duties other than just caring for Pam. All of these qualities that she demonstrated were part of the reason I wanted to marry her, and time would fail me to tell of how she broke her own health, gave up her own desire for social life, and spent herself in so many other ways to be what Pam needed so I could be what God wanted me to be.

From the very first day that we married, people began to say, "Dr. Williams, you look younger and happier than we have seen you in many years." The great weight of loneliness was lifted, and I now had a wife once again who could participate in the ministry and who could be my encourager as well as my constructive critic, and my longing to share the innermost thoughts of my heart was once more fulfilled. Every day that passes I love her more and praise the Lord for giving Jeannine to me. For the two years we have now been married, Jeannine has strived to fill the responsibilities of being the wife of Dr. Tom Williams, and God has wonderfully given her His grace to come from caretaker to wife.

In this new beginning, God has revitalized my vision to take on new projects that will enhance our service for the Lord and expand our ministry to new horizons. In so doing, He has moved me to the next level of faith to walk even now where I have not walked before, for I am now 73 years old—not 25 years old. Most men my age either falter or sit down and wait for the end. The question I posed to myself was, "Would I do this, or would I rise to new heights for God?"

Over the years I have learned that many great accomplishments have been done by men after their seventieth birthday, which included,

- Moses, who was 80 years old when God called him;
- Caleb, who was 85 when he said, "I want that mountain;"
- Michelangelo, who did his greatest work when he was 84 years old;

- Benjamin Franklin, who went as the American ambassador to England when he was 78 years old;
- Cornelius Vanderbilt, who expanded the growth of his railroads between 80 and 88 years of age; and
- Colonel Harland Sanders, who was 72 years old when he launched Kentucky Fried Chicken.

Because of these examples and others like them, I am determined that, by God's power, I can be numbered among those. We have dedicated ourselves to prayer and the stretching of our faith by adding another facet to our ministry in purchasing a beautiful 256-acre ranch in Belt, Montana, as a place where God's people can come and be helped. We are preparing to help those who have troubled marriages, and we want to major on preventative maintenance so marriages will not get in trouble.

Part of the ministry of the ranch will be to have a place for honeymoon couples to start their marriages in a godly atmosphere. We also want the ministry to encompass families' having a place to come for a truly Christian vacation. The outreach of the ranch will also include weeks for singles and for widows.

God is never in a hurry when He is building a work, and as He never rushed in my early ministry when He was building my faith and my ministry, He continues today the same. Though the property in Belgrade has not sold, which would supply the money to completely pay the debt of the new property, we still have full assurance that prayer and faith is the answer to every situation. Instead of being despondent and yielding to Satan's constant bombardment, we are marching to victory through our God because of the lessons He taught me in all the years of ministry for Him.

The Bible tells us God takes us from *faith to faith* as we travel this Christian journey for Him, and so He has continued to take me from *faith to faith* in these last two years of the new beginning He has given me. He has continued to reveal Himself as the mighty Victor over lost souls by using us to present the key to others that has opened the door to them to find hope, peace, and love through the Lord Jesus Christ.

As we moved onto the ranch in Belt, we asked our Father to make it a place where lost souls would find salvation at the foot of the Cross. How He has answered is a testament to His power to hear and His power to save. Men who have come to work on our water systems, to hook up our electric, and to deliver our propane as well as our mail have bowed their heads receiving the One Who is able to deliver them from darkness to light and from eternal damnation to eternal life.

When our sprinkler system was not working correctly, two men came to check on and clear out the pipes because the water is drawn from the creek that flows alongside the property. When I posed the question, "Do you know if Heaven will be your home?" to both of them, one answered, "Yes, I have been saved through Christ." However, the other one said, "No, I didn't know you could be certain." After sharing Scripture with him about how he could be certain of having a home in Heaven, he bowed his head and received Christ. We all three rejoiced with the angels in Heaven that another one entered into the fold!

As Jeannine and I were traveling home from a meeting, we stopped to fill the car with gas and had the privilege to lead a young lady working in the combined convenience store to the Lord. She listened with such intent and, with tears in her eyes, came to know Christ as her own. It has been a continued joy to behold God's amazing salvation wrought in so many lives.

God continues to use His Word to guide us along the path He has for us as He did when He moved us from Belgrade to Belt. As I have said in an earlier chapter, God used a car wreck to get me to obey Him and fly to my meetings, and since 2002 He has asked me not to fly—for what reason only God knows. I have just obeyed. While we were still in Belgrade, we realized we were going to be traveling by car and by train to meetings, so I believed God was directing us to leave Belgrade and move to the Great Falls area about three and one-half hours north. When I posed this possibility to Jeannine, she was willing to follow but was hesitant about leaving as she had become so fond of the Bozeman area, the people, and the mountains that enveloped the city. She knew the Great Falls area was a more plains-style of terrain, though there are mountains that could be seen in the distance. God had used the mountains to be such a source of comfort and strength to her.

One morning during her prayer and Bible reading, God directed her attention to Deuteronomy 2:3 which says, *"Ye have compassed this mountain long enough: turn you northward."* God had led her to be as sure as I was that He was directing us north to Great Falls. We moved to Great Falls and began homesteading at the K.O.A. campground in the motor home. Neither of our houses had sold yet, and God spoke to my heart and asked, "Do the houses have to be sold for you to obey and move north?" God was teaching me another level of faith.

The Lord has a perfect plan that He unfolds to us bit by bit, and He is never in a hurry. In His mercy He protected us from two pieces of property that we, in our eagerness to receive His blueprint, sought to pursue. In His perfect time, He led us to the beautiful ranch I described earlier in this chapter. We were driving east to a meeting when He opened our eyes to the town of Belt. Jeannine was driving so I could get some phone calling completed; it was spring, and the fields and foothills were a lush green which captivated her attention. As she drove along this route, she happened to look left, and God opened a narrow window, revealing a town nestled in the valley. We have since driven that route many times, but unless you are aware of the exact location and know when to look, the town is not viewable from the road. She whispered a silent prayer and said, "Oh, Lord, this is beautiful. I wouldn't mind living out this way."

At our first meeting on this trip, God spoke to me that He wanted me to think of a larger work than I had been thinking of for Him to do with our ministry, and as I shared this with Jeannine, she said, "God spoke to me tonight about the same thing." Then she told me what God had revealed to her as we drove out of Great Falls. We had our realtor begin looking for "ranch"-size property in that area when we returned, and God led us to the place on Belt Creek Road. He miraculously moved us onto the property six months later, using one of our board members, Rusty Mooreland. Brother Rusty and his wife Sandy said, "God laid on our hearts to provide the down payment of $250,000 as a loan to the ministry with zero percent interest and no payment due until the place in Belgrade sold."

God took me to another level of faith during this time to believe Him to provide as the house in Belgrade was yet unsold. He sold Jeannine's house that she had owned in Belgrade, and we closed on her house the same day we closed on the Belt ranch. God's glory has been abundant as He has delayed the selling of the Belgrade property. He has shown me it isn't that I have great faith but that I have faith in a mighty and great God! He has a plan that He will reveal and unfold as His timing presents itself to be perfect.

While we have been waiting for God's perfect timing, He has wonderfully supplied each month for all our financial needs—whether through one large gift given or through taking the little we had and making it enough. We have increased our schedule of meetings as we wait by praying for God to send them. We have once more experienced the power of God during these travels. We were traveling through Tennessee and had pulled into an R.V. park a couple of

hours outside of Knoxville when the next morning God opened up
an opportunity for me to share the power of salvation with a gentleman. He had walked over to our motor home where we were secur-
ing our car onto the trailer and began a very pleasant conversation.
He was an avid Tennessee Volunteer football fan and was on his way
to watch one of their games. After hearing of the great love of our
Saviour and that he too could come to know Him, he eagerly bowed
his head and asked Christ to be his. When we arrived in the
Knoxville area later that day, we were told the Volunteers were on
an away game and weren't playing at home until the next week. The
man's mix-up was God's plan to win him to the Saviour.

While we were in Pigeon Forge preaching a meeting, God used
us to be a channel of blessing to another pastor and his wife who
were seeking rest in that area for health reasons. God guided our
paths that day to meet up not only once, but multiple times, and
then He took the message that night to encourage the hearts of
these dear servants of His.

While God was supplying the financial needs for the property
payments, general bills, payroll taxes and the salary for our employees, there wasn't enough for us to continue receiving a salary. He
stretched our faith once again from April until December 2008, and
in so doing, it was glorious to watch Him provide our personal needs.

We were traveling to Connecticut when Jeannine noticed a dark
black lesion on my neck. I am susceptible to skin cancer and have
had a number of places removed, one time requiring the Mohs treat-
ment. For me, finding a dark, black lesion is an automatic sign stating that immediate action is required.

We called ahead to the pastor in Connecticut; however, he was
unable to schedule an appointment to see a doctor. Jeannine's pas-

tor from her years in Connecticut attended the meeting and told me he could get me in the next day to see his doctor. We didn't have the money, but we believed God to provide and, at the same time, asked Him to make the place benign. The doctor was very thorough in his examination and told us, "I do not believe the place is cancerous, but I'm not 100 percent sure. I recommend you have it removed and sent to a lab to be sure." He referred me to an area dermatologist, and I was able to schedule an appointment for the following week, which worked well as we were remaining to preach at the Lighthouse Baptist Church in Norwalk where Jeannine had attended so many years previously.

The dermatologist we were referred to was one of God's chosen people, a Jew, and God opened a wonderful door of opportunity to talk to him about Christ. His assistant and the lady who was in charge of the scheduling and office department, we learned, were children of the King as our conversation with them revealed this. We shared with them the tremendous outpouring of the Holy Spirit we had experienced in the recent meeting, and they shared their concern for the doctor's need of salvation. The doctor had been in and out of the examining room during our conversation with these ladies, and as he walked in to remove the place on my neck, he said, "I see you don't have insurance."

"No, I don't have insurance because the Lord asked me not to over 40 years ago." I then added, "I understand that you are a Jew."

"Yes, I am," he replied.

I told him, "My best friend is a Jew."

He said, "Well, there are lots of us around."

"Yes, but this Jew is more special than any others," I told him.

"Oh, how is that?" he asked.

"His name is Jesus, and He died that we might know Heaven as our home," I answered.

see many family members, immediate and extended, more than once. He also allowed us to visit a long-time college friend of hers who had given birth to a baby boy with only half of his heart functioning properly. We were able to spend time with her as an encouragement through fellowship and prayer, which she told us was a great blessing to her and her husband. Other similar opportunities have been opened to us as well as we travel across this nation, not by air but by the multiple freeway systems of our country.

Journeying from *faith to faith* is a road difficult, at times, to travel, but a road that is well worth traveling as God reveals more and more of His mighty great power! As Charles H. Spurgeon wrote, "Look not so much to thy hand with which thou art grasping Christ, as to Christ; look not to thy hope, but to Jesus, the source of thy hope; look not to thy faith, but to Jesus, the author and finisher of thy faith; it is what Jesus is, not what we are, that gives rest to the soul."

The road you are called to travel for the Lord may not be the same as our road, but our Heavenly Father will be there to guide you, to keep you, and to help you as our Saviour sits at the right hand of the throne interceding for you. If we can remember to live our days one at a time by prayer and by faith, we will discover the truth of Matthew 11:30, *"For my yoke is easy, and my burden is light."*

"Oh, that Jew," he said with a little chuckle, as he turned to his assistant and said, "You probably are enjoying this."

She answered, "You need to listen to what he is saying."

Once he had cut the place off my neck, he turned to his assistant and told her, "You make the call."

She called the lab where the specimen was being sent and told them the doctor would be writing this one off as a tax deduction. He had paid for our entire lab expense.

As we walked to the front of the office to pay the bill for the office visit, the other lady said, "You don't owe us anything, Dr. Williams. It was a privilege to meet you and your wife and hear all that God is doing through your ministry. Please pray for him to be saved," referring to the dermatologist.

God allowed us to meet two sisters in Christ, witness to one of His chosen, and watch Him so easily provide for our needs. This was a demonstration that we simply have faith in a mighty and great God, as He also answered our prayer when we received the call telling us the place on my neck was not cancerous.

As we wound our way back toward Montana, we were in North Carolina finishing our last meeting for this particular trip. That night at supper, Jeannine felt something hard as she bit into some meat. Upon further investigation, she found a crown had come off her tooth. The pastor's wife was able to schedule an appointment at their dentist office for early the next morning. She also went with us to the appointment, and as we went up to pay, she intercepted the bill and said, "No, Dr. Williams, my husband told me to pay for it." God continued to meet personal needs in just the same wonderful way through His children that walked in obedience to His will.

⤳⤳

Traveling has also afforded us blessings we might otherwise not have encountered had we been flying instead of driving. During our travels across the country, He has allowed us to visit family and spend holidays with them because we have been near where they live as we drove from one meeting to another.

Jeannine's family had a very large family reunion planned the summer of 2008 for all the extended members to gather and visit— something that hadn't happened in a number of years. It was planned for the Saturday before we were to begin meetings that following Sunday in Connecticut, and the reunion was held in California. We thought we could get her a plane ticket out of New York (God had only asked **me** not to fly) in time to be at the reunion and then back for the week of meetings. This way she would only have to miss the Sunday services in Connecticut; however, as she prayed, she knew that God wanted her in Connecticut, not California. During the invitation of the Sunday evening service in Connecticut, the pastor asked Jeannine to deal with the spiritual needs of a lady who had come forward. God wonderfully used Jeannine to fulfill the doubts this lady had concerning her salvation as they read the Scriptures and spoke together.

The lady said, "I've come forward a number of times because I'm just not sure I'm saved."

As the lady shared her story with my wife, Jeannine prayed, "God give me the words. You know her heart and what she needs to hear from You." God did give her the words, and when she finished speaking, the lady with a very joyful countenance said, "It clicked! I understand! Thank you so much!" That dear lady went home that evening with peace and assurance and a radiance that expressed she indeed was saved. It was such an encouragement to Jeannine because she was very disappointed to have missed the family reunion.

God honored her obedience to Him; and that autumn as we traveled through California on a preaching tour, He allowed her to